DAVE ALBER: TRAVEL ART 2018: PART 1: INTIMATIONS

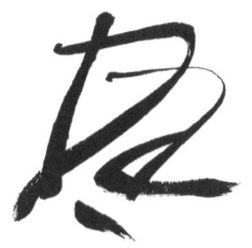

Contemporary American Expatriate
Painter Series

CONTEMPORARY AMERICAN EXPATRIATE PAINTER SERIES

C

4 *Short Biography*

5 *Statement*

6 *Article: A Brief Introduction to Chinese Temples*

7 *Painting: Approaching Dongwu Temple on Chinese New Years Eve (Suzhou, China)*

8 *Painting: Nepalese Tongba (Jaand or Millet Beer) (Kathmandu, Nepal)*

9 *Painting: Little Tiger at the Fruit Stand (Suzhou, China)*

10 *Article: The Floral Mandarin Fish*

11 *Painting: Cooking Mandarin Fish (Gue Yu)*

12 *Painting: Bupaya Pagoda, Bagan, Myanmar (Burma)*

13 *Painting: Bund in Shanghai, China, in Front of the Custom House (Clock Tower)*

14–19 *Article: Ancestors and Immortals: a Foreigner's Introduction to Ching Ming Festival*

15 *Painting: Burning Joss Paper During Ching Ming Festival*

17 *Painting: Paper Mansion For Ancestors During Ching Ming Festival*

ISBN-10: 1724953346
ISBN-13: 978-1724953346

Contemporary American Expatriate Painter Series

DAVE ALBER: TRAVEL ART 2018: PART 1: INTIMATIONS

ontents

19	Painting: Lady He (He Xiangu) of the Eight Immortals
20	Painting: Chinese Garuda
21–23	Comic: Bedding Shanghai
24	Painting: Suzhou Center Mall in the Rain, East Side
25	Painting: Suzhou Center Mall in the Rain, East Entrance
26	Article: Getting Social at Suzhou's Night Market
27	Painting: Eating With Friends at Dachengfang Guanqian Night Market, Suzhou, China
28	Painting: "WAIGUARAN!"
29	Painting: Dushu Lake Church (Suzhou, China)
30	Painting: Peacock Window (Bhaktapur, Nepal)
31	Painting: Dave Alber, Self-Portrait at Swayambunath, Kathmandu, Nepal
32	Portrait Paintings in Chinese Ink

Contact Dave on WeChat or DaveAlber.com

Copyright © 2018 Dave Alber.
All rights reserved.
Newspaper and magazine reproductions
© the respective publisher and reproduced
with their consent.

www.DaveAlber.com

Short Biography

Dave Alber was educated extensively in the Humanities: practicing and studying the fine arts at the University of West Georgia (BFA) and studying mythology at Pacifica Graduate Institute (MA). For twenty years he earned a living as an illustrator and graphic designer. Yet, he felt a deep desire to live abroad, travel regularly, and enjoy rich new cultural experiences every day.

He sold most of his belongings and booked a flight to Kathmandu, Nepal, where — *when not visiting historic temples, celebrating raucous festivals, and hiking through the Himalayan foothills* — he developed *The Rhythm of Health: Post-Traumatic Stress Education and Relaxation Training Program*® for suffering soldiers. While teaching at the university level and traveling in Costa Rica, Saudi Arabia, and China, he developed the *Easy American Accent*® brand of English learning products.

Along the way he published a book of poetry, *To the Dawn*, a book about art, *Myth & Medium*, a novel, *Alien Sex in Silicon Valley*, and a global anthology of world mythology, *The Heart of Myth: Wisdom Stories from Endangered Peoples*.

In time, he asked himself how art and writing could best connect with people directly to share the florescence of the diverse human experience across the globe. With this purpose, he began painting **Travel Art** and publishing travel writing. Presently, he sells his paintings locally in Suzhou, China (the art capital of the Ming and Qing Dynasties), on Chinese social media, and **DaveAlber.com** where his **Travel Art Adventurer's Club** offers exclusive deals, discounts on commissioned work, portrait painting, and special invitations to fine art auctions.

Statement

"The images in **Intimations** are **Travel Art** painted with the intent to connect with others and share a mutual — *and mirror-like* — sense of wonder and joy within this world we inhabit. Paintings depict people, temples, cityscapes, food and drink, rituals of remembrance, and celebrations of friendship. The images are of the world we share… together.

Painting in a neo-expressionist and colorist approach, I attempt to invoke or "call forth" an experience of that mutually reflective magical quality of an intense presence within an aesthetic frame occupied by people and objects in a rich environment pulsing with life.

These paintings are subjective and immersive, often layered or highly textured, and painted with a kaleidoscopic burst of colors, all with the intent to convey a palpable life-force energy, which might invade the viewer's experience from the, often intentionally flattened, picture plane.

Thus, the flat-world of the apparent picture plane is transcended like the illusion of dream by the invocation of intimations — *glimpses of light* — as eyes blink themselves into wakefulness."

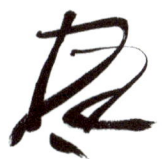

CONTEMPORARY AMERICAN EXPATRIATE PAINTER SERIES

A brief introduction to Chinese temples

By Dave Alber

Last week, I went to Shanghai to meet a friend visiting from the United States. After having lunch together, we walked to the Shanghai City God Temple. Although I've become accustomed to Chinese temples, having lived in China for four years, my friend was surprised by the multitude of banners, deity icons, incense offerings, and the rhythmic chanting of the monks. "It's a bit overwhelming," he said, taking a seat. "It's baroque in its complexity, but totally alien to me in its iconography. I can't make heads or tales of it." Inspired by my friend's confusion, I decided to write a brief introduction to Chinese temples.

Chinese temples are commonly of three varieties, Buddhist, Taoist, or for Chinese folk religion. That said, many temple complexes are syncretic, in that, although they predominantly represent one of the above three traditions, they also contain shrines for other traditions. For example, Suzhou's Dongwu Si Temple is emphatically Buddhist, however it contains a large shrine room of folk icons for folk religious services.

Upon visiting a Chinese temple, how are visitors to distinguish whether a temple is Buddhist, Taoist, or for Chinese folk religion? Start by looking at the names. When looking at the names of the temples, miao refers to a folk temple; guan refers to a Taoist temple or monastery; and si refers to a Chinese Buddhist temple. When examining a temple's appearance, one

Author bio:
Dave Alber is the author of *To the Dawn, Myth & Medium,* and *Alien Sex in Silicon Valley.* His book *The Heart of Myth* is a global anthology of living myth that unpacks the grammar of world mythology. His Travel Art can be found at DaveAlber.com.

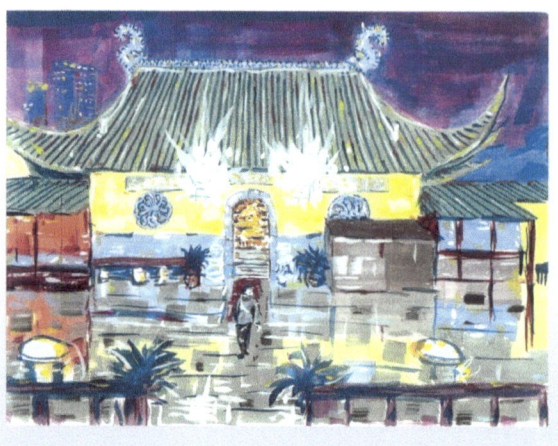

finds that Buddhist temples are often (but not always) red and gold, while Taoist temples are often (but not always) more subdued in color with shades of greys. Upon entering the temple, the visitor should notice the people operating the temple. Are they dressed as monks or wearing a premodern uniform? Buddhist monks' robes are often yellow, gold, red, tan, or grey. While Taoist priests wear an outfit that is often grey, blue, and black, but is most identifiable as being a religious uniform from China's dynastic period.

Buddhism is complex, and Buddhist temples in China are representative of three stages of the religion's history. In its 2500 year history, Buddhism has gone off in several different directions: the original monastic Buddhism is Theravada; the popular icon-rich polytheistic Buddhism is Hinayana, the uniquely Chinese Taoist-influenced Buddhism is Chan (Zen in Japan); and the Buddhism indigenous to the Tibetan region is Vajrayana. That said, the Buddhist temples you will see in China are predominantly Chinese Hinayana with some Theravada temples found mostly in Tibet and western Yunan and Sichuan.

What are some examples of the three types of Chinese temples (Taoist, Buddhist, and folk religion) within Suzhou? Some great examples of Chinese temples can be experienced in one day starting in Leqiao, the center of Suzhou's old city. In the very center of Leqiao, the enigmatically named Temple of Mystery (Xuanmiaoguan) is an impressive Taoist temple. West of Leqiao, on the north side of Jingde Road is the Chenghuang Miao temple, Suzhou's City god temple. South of Leqiao, on Chuanxin Street, is the Baoguo Si Temple, a Chan Buddhist temple, which offers a unique glimpse into China's contribution to the flavor of Buddhism. Going beyond the three most common examples of temple types, south of Leqiao, on Renmin Road, Suzhou even offers a Confucian temple, a large red temple honoring China's greatest teacher. Differentiating itself from the three previous temple-types, it is slightly more restrained in its iconography. It's surrounding garden is calm and peaceful, a welcome escape from the overwhelm one may experience when encountering the complexity of China's temples.

"A Brief Introduction to Chinese Temples" is an article published in the Suzhou Review on April 9, 2018. **Approaching Dongwu Temple on Chinese New Years Eve (Suzhou, China)** is a gouache illustration featured in the article.

Suzhou Review can be found at all Suzhou newstands and on WeChat.

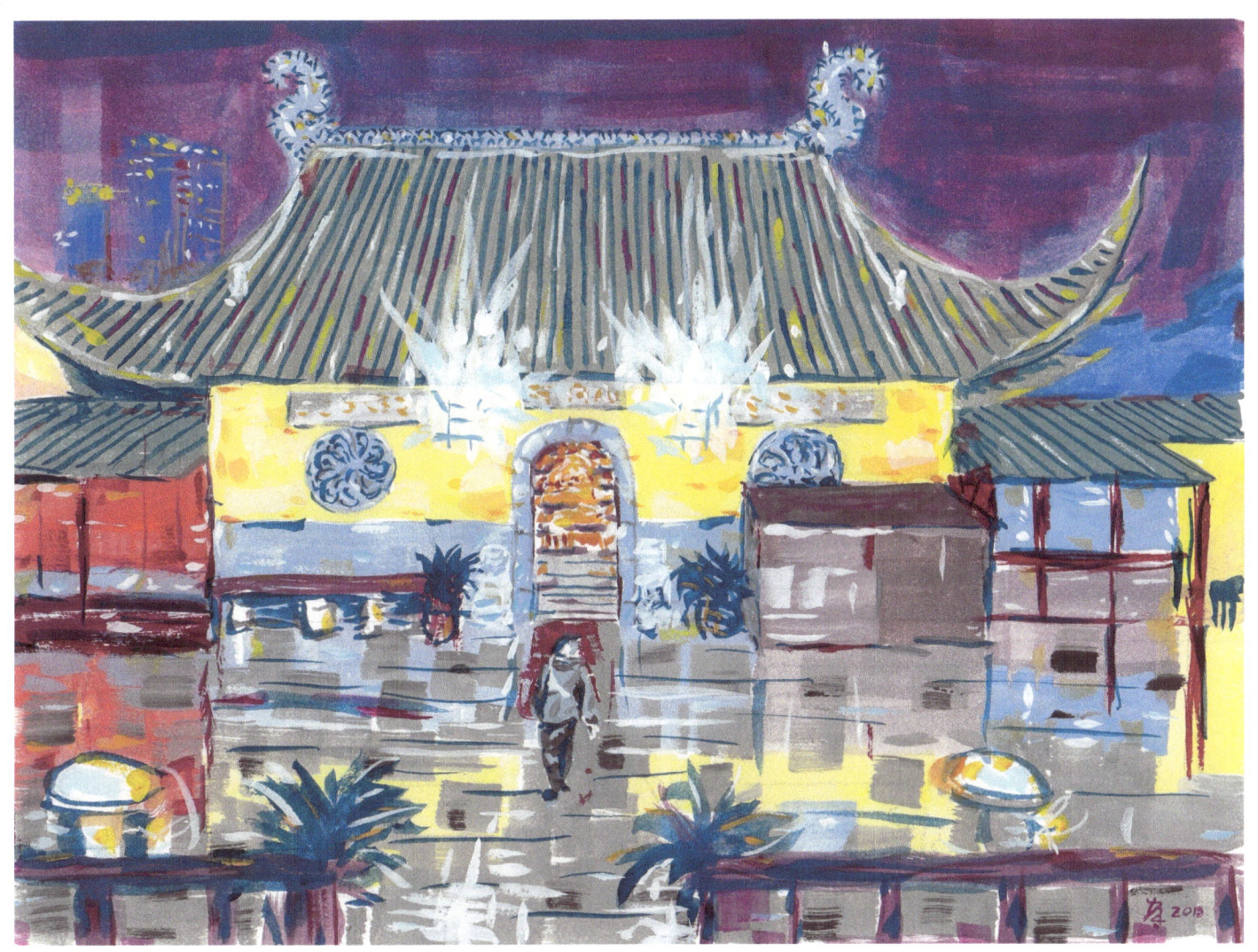

Approaching Dongwu Temple on Chinese New Years Eve (Suzhou, China)

2018
Gouache on paper
7.4 x 9.6 in.   (18.8 x 24.38 cm.)

CONTEMPORARY AMERICAN EXPATRIATE PAINTER SERIES

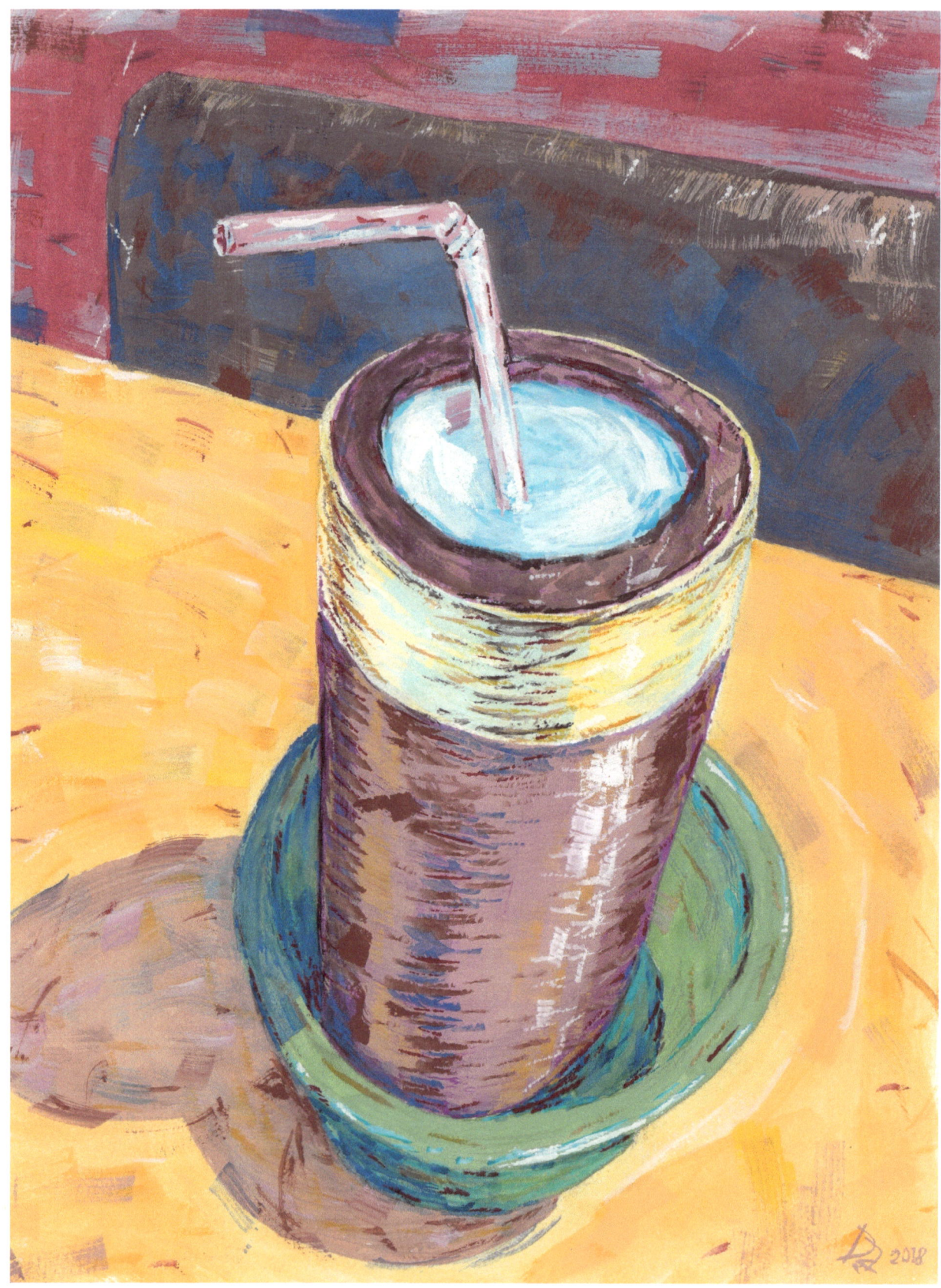

Nepalese Tongba (Jaand or Millet Beer) (Kathmandu, Nepal)

2018
Gouache on paper
7.4 x 9.6 in.   (18.8 x 24.38 cm.)

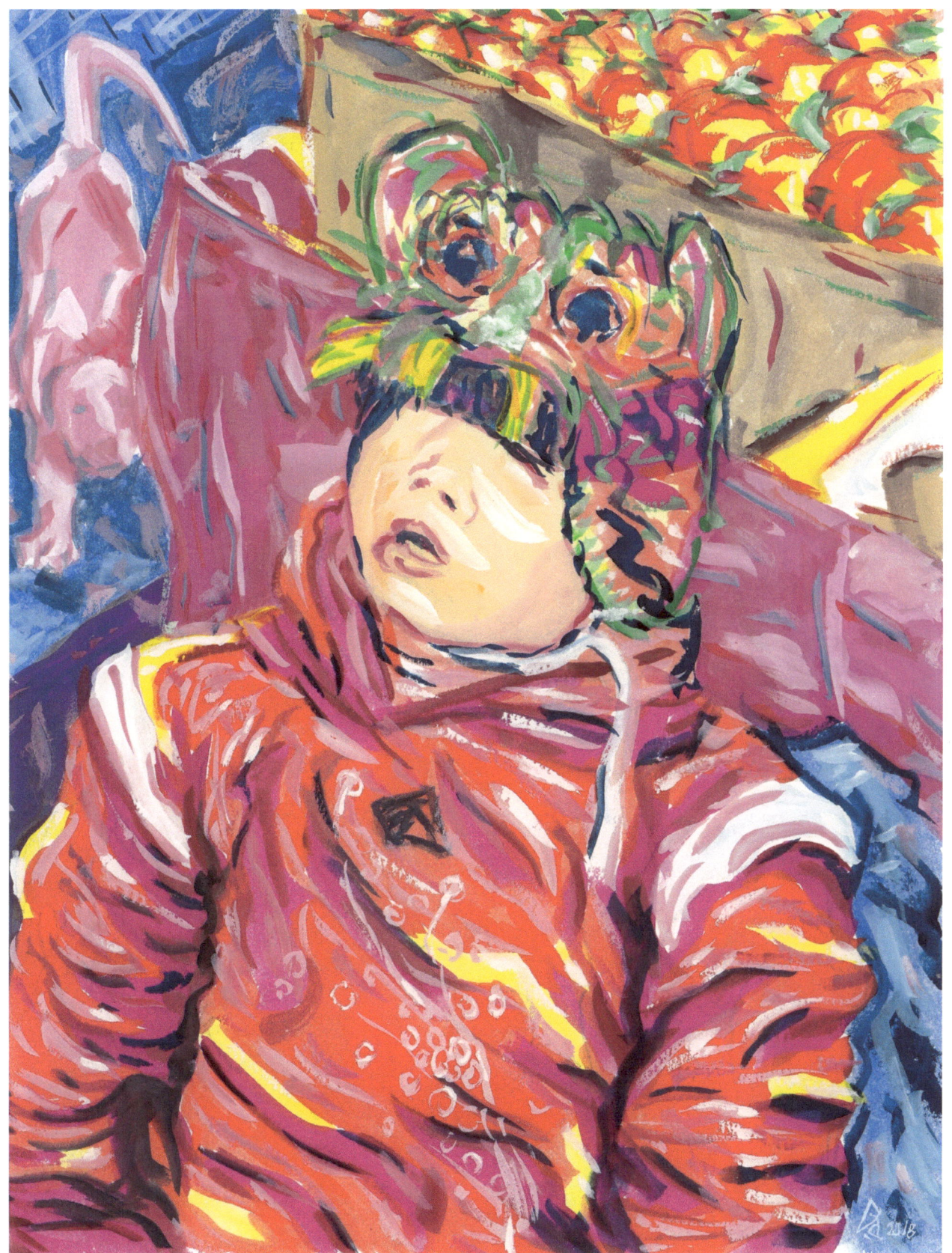

Little Tiger at the Fruit Stand (Suzhou, China)

2018
Gouache on paper
7.4 x 9.6 in.   (18.8 x 24.38 cm.)

CONTEMPORARY AMERICAN EXPATRIATE PAINTER SERIES

"The Floral Mandarin Fish" is an article published in the Suzhou Review on May 14, 2018. **Cooking Mandarin Fish (Gue Yu)** is a gouache illustration featured in the article.

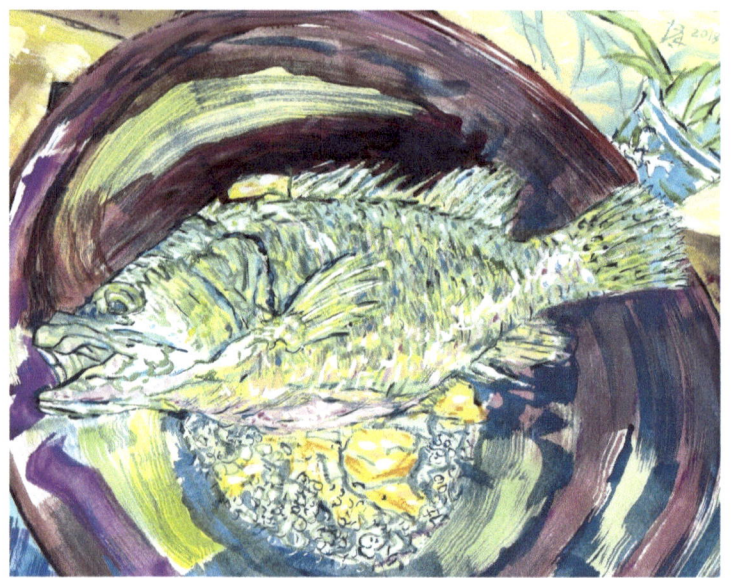

The floral mandarin fish

Article and Picture by Dave Alber

The Chinese perch is known by different names. In the West, it is one of the several fish known imprecisely as the mandarin fish. Its biological taxonomy in Latin is siniperca chuatsi, which translates to Chinese perch (sini-perca.) In Chinese, it is known as gui yu, which translates to "banded fish with a bulge on its back", or as gui hua yu, "banded flower fish", I have been told, owing to its beauty.[i] As one of Suzhou's most popular dishes, it can be found in most fish restaurants in Suzhou as song shu gui yu or "squirrel fish".

Squirrel fish is the most popular and certainly the most flamboyant method of preparing the fish. A sweet and sour dish, the first thing you'll notice when the fish is brought to your table at a restaurant, is that it is bright orange. Also, it is served whole, head and all, and presented magnificently, belly-down, head arched upward, open-mouthed. Its body seems exaggerated in size due to its flesh being covered in fry-battered spikes of meat. At the rear, its tail appears to be a broad brightly spotted fan. Taken in as a whole, lying in a pool of sweet and sour sauce, and garnished with pieces of pineapple, the squirrel fish is exciting in its otherworldly appearance and sweet fragrance.

Without doubt, squirrel fish is delicious. But all said, it is an almost over-the-top, even outrageous, way to serve a naturally delicious fish. I say this because frying a fish and covering it in a sweet and sour sauce isn't exactly the best way to express its natural flavor, and the natural flavor of this white lake perch is exceptionally unique! In my estimation steaming it is the best way to truly bring out the natural flavor of the flesh, skin, and broth. The first time I had mandarin fish steamed was at a Christmas party where I have to admit — with a shame similar to that of forgetting a host's name at a party — I did not recognize the fish as that same fish who's company I had enjoyed earlier in the week as squirrel fish. That steamed Christmas fish in the center of the table was uniquely delicious. The fish's skin had puffed up and with the meat connecting it, became soft, somewhat gelatinous in texture, and was surprisingly fragrant. When people say that they don't like fish, it's usually because they find the "fishy" smell to be somewhat off-putting to them. Not so the mandarin fish. When steamed in its own juices, its meat has a surprisingly delicate fragrant flavor. I hadn't experienced anything like it before.

After discovering the fish's name — gui yu — I felt like a culinary prince who had found his Cinderella, and I was determined to try my hand at preparing the mandarin fish served, as I had had it at that Christmas party, steamed in its own juices.

You can do this yourself by using either a steamer or a wok if you do the stir-fry steam method. To prepare it in this technique, you'll need to gut the mandarin fish, and let it sit in a marinade of yellow cooking wine, soy sauce, and salt for a few hours. You'll also need to cut fresh ginger into small slices. The cooking is easy and quick. First, heat a small amount of oil in the wok, quickly warming the fish on both sides. Then making sure to be careful of the hot oil, pour in the marinade with a little water and cover the wok to allow the fish to steam in this broth. Flip the fish and recover the wok, checking both the level of water in the wok and the softness of the meat. When the meat is soft and tender, garnish it with green onions, steaming them for about thirty seconds, and then finally pouring the fish and its broth into a shallow bowl, which you can serve to family and friends at the table.

I'm sure your guests will comment on the unique fragrance of the gui yu, or as it is also known gui hua yu ("banded flower fish".) Perhaps there is a play on words here, for isn't another meaning for gui "sweet smelling flower"? " Maybe the mandarin fish isn't called "flower fish" due to its elegant good looks alone, but also due to the unique floral fragrance of its meat.

Author bio:
Dave Alber is a fine artist in Suzhou, China and the author of *To the Dawn, Myth & Medium*, and *Alien Sex in Silicon Valley*. His book *Heart of Myth* is a global anthology of living myth that unpacks the grammar of world mythology. His *Travel Art* can be found at DaveAlber.com and in China at ArtAnd.cn.

i 花 hua = flower.
ii 厥 gui = band, which is the right side of the character 鳜, gui yu or "banded fish". 桂 gui = sweet smelling flower.

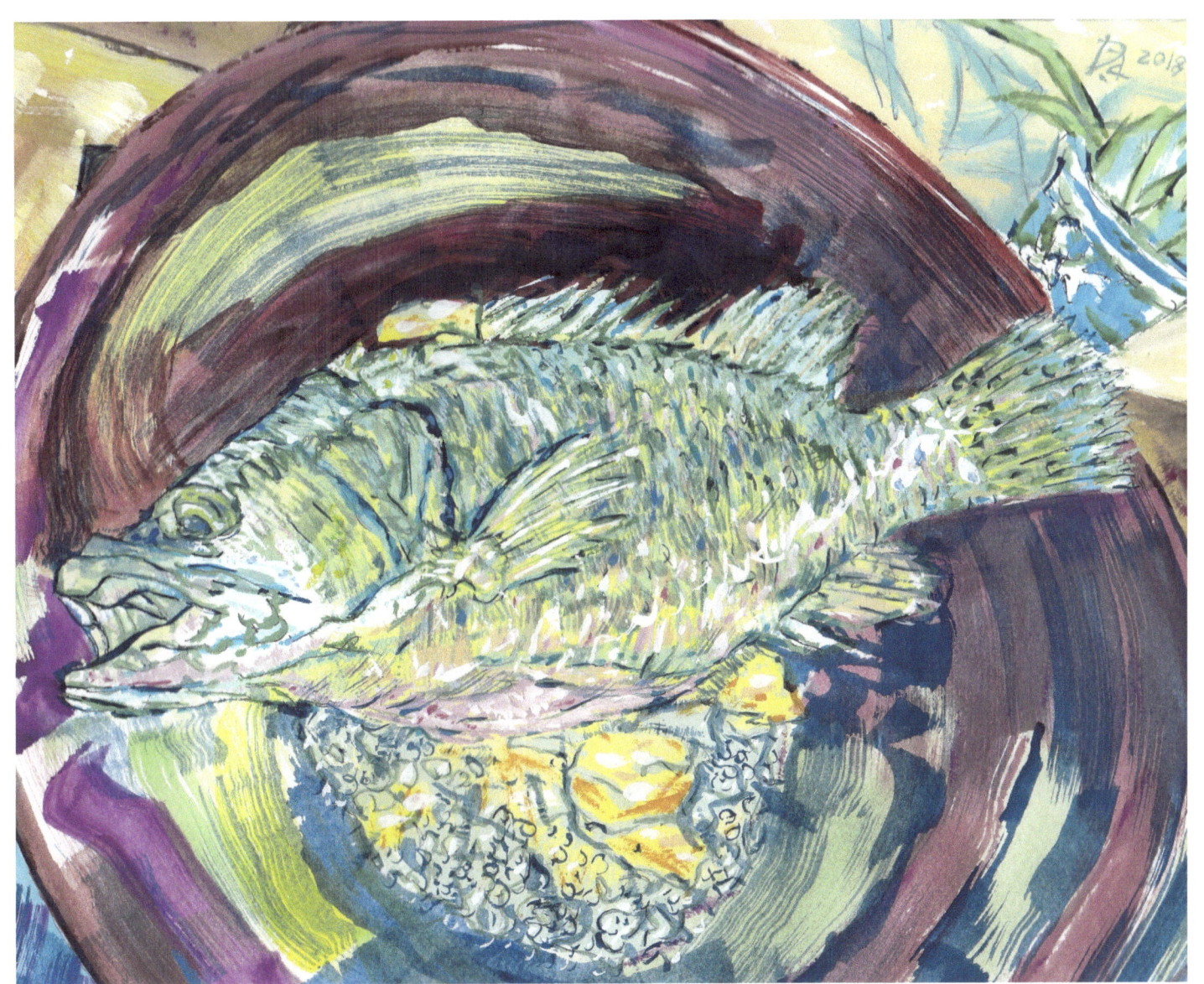

Cooking Mandarin Fish (Gue Yu)

2018
Gouache on paper
10 x 7 in.   (23.5 x 17.15 cm.)

CONTEMPORARY AMERICAN EXPATRIATE PAINTER SERIES

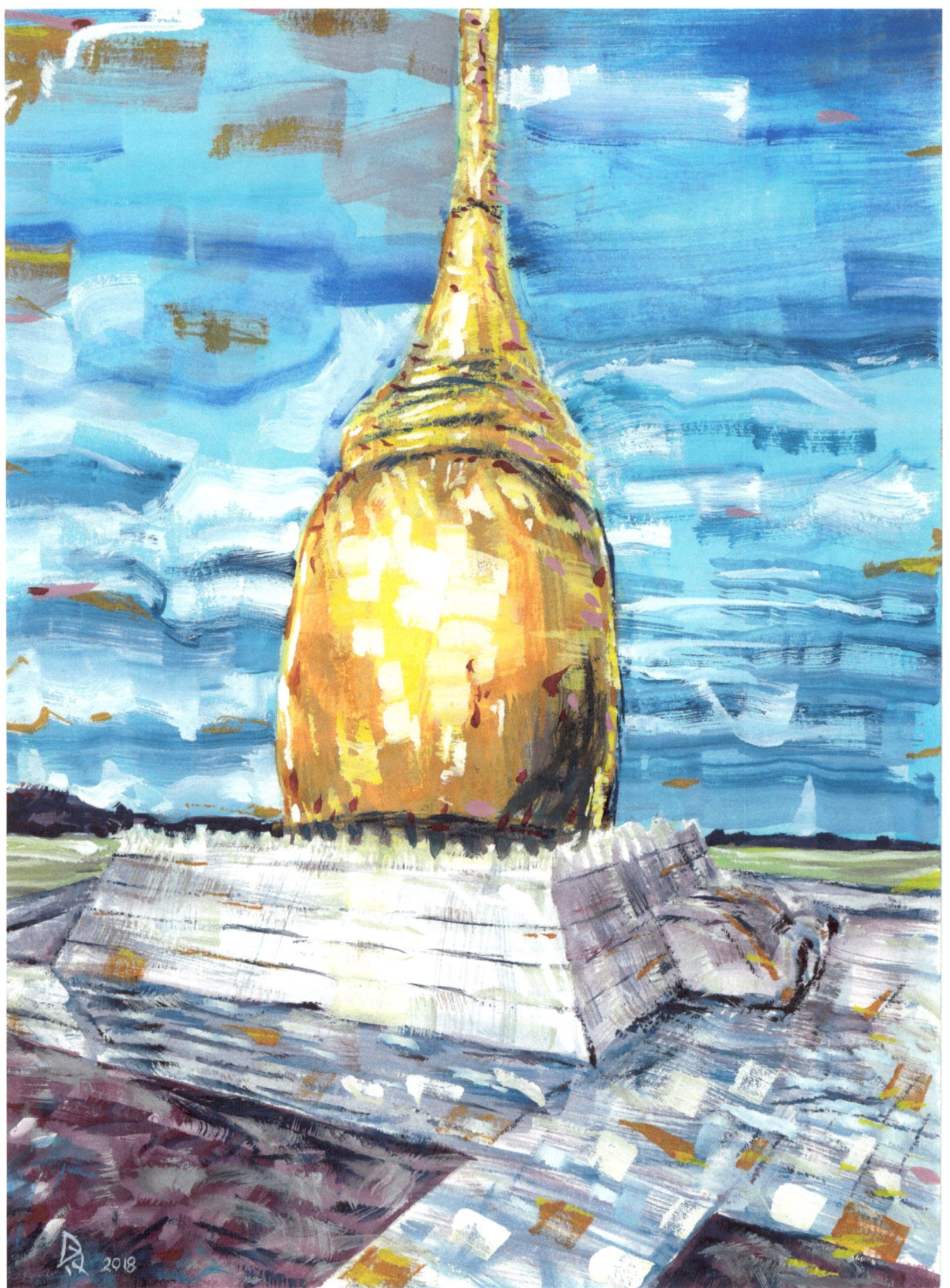

Bupaya Pagoda, Bagan, Myanmar (Burma)

2018
Gouache on paper
7.4 x 9.6 in.   (18.8 x 24.38 cm.)

DAVE ALBER: TRAVEL ART 2018: PART 1: INTIMATIONS

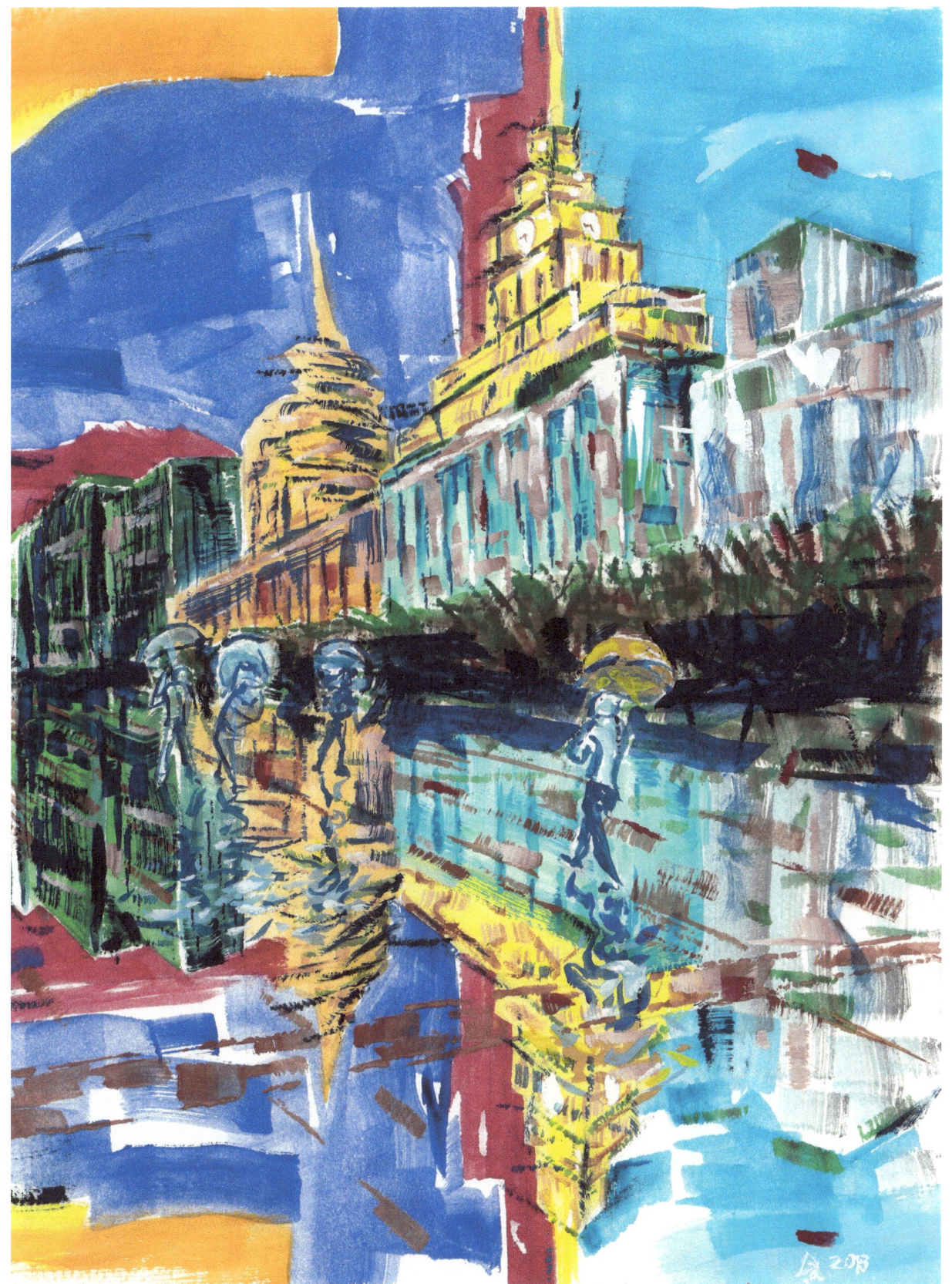

Bund in Shanghai, China, in Front of the Custom House (Clock Tower)

2018
Gouache on paper
7.4 x 9.6 in.   (18.8 x 24.38 cm.)

CONTEMPORARY AMERICAN EXPATRIATE PAINTER SERIES

"Ancestors and Immortals: a Foreigner's Introduction to Ching Ming Festival" appeared in Suzhou, China's **OPEN magazine**, issue 138, April 2018. The article contained three paintings.

You can get free **OPEN magazine** in five-star hotels, high-end restaurants and clubs and foreign supermarkets, international schools and private clubs in Suzhou-Wuxi-Changzhou area. You can browse the OPEN electronic journals on WeChat.

OPEN Wechat QR Code

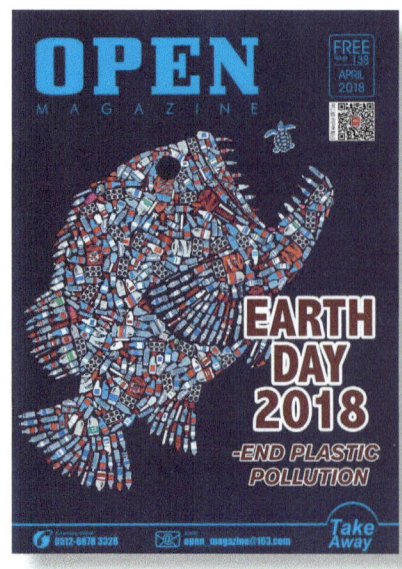

Ancestors and Immortals: a Foreigner's Introduction to Ching Ming Festival

He Wen Ping is marvelous. His house is decorated wall to wall with pages from the Song Dynasty Three Character Classic for his toddling son to practice his Chinese. Thus, his son practices at an early age such Confucian sayings as:

> 高曾祖，父而身。
> 身而子，子而孫。
> 自子孫，至玄曾。
> 乃九族，人之倫。

In English:

> Great great grandfather, great grandfather,
>   grandfather,
> father and self,
> self and son,
> son and grandson,
> from son and grandson
> on to great grandson and great great
>   grandson.
> These are the nine patrilineal relationships, constituting the kinships of man.

Wen Ping asked some of his English friends to participate in his family's traditional Ching Ming celebrations. My friend Bill and I were fortunate enough to be able to accept. So bright and early April 4th, Wen Ping and family picked us up in a rented SUV. We drove out of the Henan city of Jiaozuo to a nearby small town where Wen Ping's family gravesite is located.

People all across China would be visiting ancestral graves this day because Ching Ming Festival is a Chinese holiday honoring family ancestors. The holiday falls on the 1st day of the 5th solar term of the Asian lunisolar calendar. In English it is known as Tomb Sweeping Day. On this national holiday people clean and repair ancestral gravesites and make offerings of food, wine, paper clothing, and fake money.

Wen Ping's rented SUV parked at the end of a country road alongside other vehicles. We greeted Wen Ping's brothers and sisters and their families and walked single file on an elevated path between damp clay fields filled with green wheatgrass swaying in the wind.

The gravesite consisted of several unobtrusive unmarked mounds in the middle of the wheat field. Almost immediately the ceremony began. There wasn't any leader. People had done this their whole lives, so everyone knew what to do. Food was placed on the mounds and colored joss paper, clothes, and money were burned at each mound. The offerings were made in a sequence according to family rank; eldest to

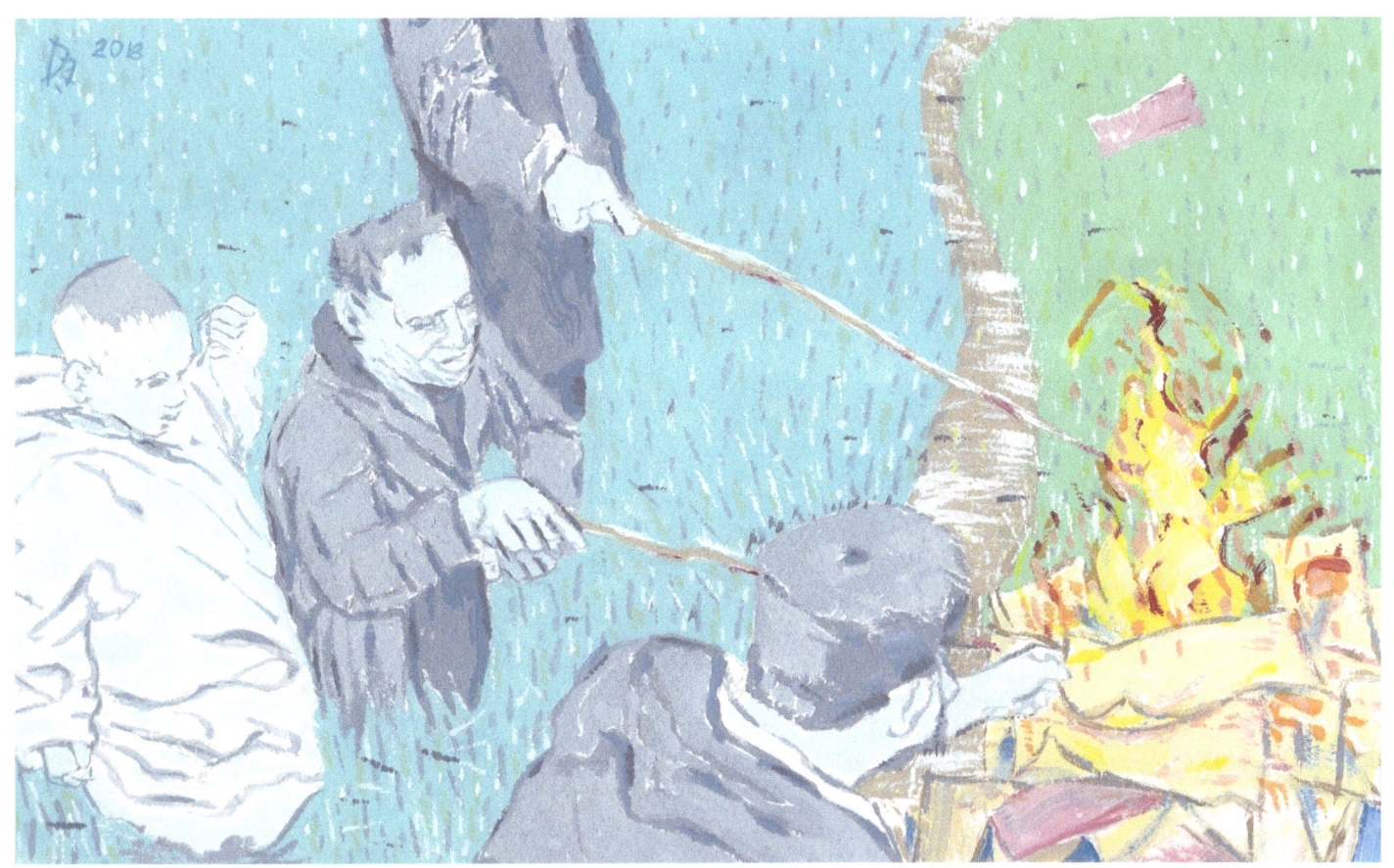

Burning Joss Paper During Ching Ming Festival

2018
Gouache on paper
9.625 x 5.75 in. (24.44 x 14.6 cm.)

youngest, male to female. The ritual was simple and elegant. Wen Ping explained as Bill and I observed the process and kneeled and bowed at the appropriate times. "This is my father. This is my mother and this one here is my grandfather."

As this was all consistent with what I had read about the festival, I assumed that the holiday was more or less over. However, I couldn't have been more wrong. For the holiday, the ceremonies, and the fuller extent of ancestor devotion was to unpack more richness, color and surprises than I had anticipated.

We went back to the small town and piled out of the SUV. Wen Ping went into a house and met with extended family. Bill and I walked down the street to listen to some musicians who had set up loudspeakers along the thin dusty alley. It seemed like KTV (Chinese Karaoke) village style. We played the role of foreign celebrities and chatted and posed with the locals as their friends took cell phone pictures. Wen Ping came for us, and to my surprise, the whole assembly, musicians and all, marched in a long parade to another field. This one had many gravestones and piles of huge paper mansions, cars, televisions, and luxury goods. Long strings of firecrackers were draped on the trees. The musicians played the erhu (a stringed instrument); stick percussion; and cymbals, all improvised around a gourd-like wind instrument that sounded something like a high-pitched bagpipe.

Pointing at the graves, Wen Ping explained, "These are our village ancestors. That one over there is the oldest."

Everyone in this village was more or less related. This truly was a village in the most traditional sense of the word. The village was essentially a clan. We were all at the gravesite to honor shared clan ancestors. Huge piles of joss paper and money were burned. I pitched in to help with the fires. Surprising flash bonfires of paper mansions ignited and then disappeared in seconds. Firecrackers exploded around us. The honking clamor of festival music was an elevated drone holding the event firmly in ritual space.

Fires burned all around us. And what really is fire? A thing? In Asia, and many traditional cultures around the world, fire is a medium between worlds. It is a process that links the world of objective daylight reality with the subtle and invisible worlds of the dead. And what are the worlds of the dead? Way stations; transitional depots; ethereal realms; natural processes of ecology; archetypical Chinese bureaucracies; places where the deceased learn to shed desires for the transient objects of the sunlit world; locations where the deceased have their personalities mirrored back to them; and heavens and hells in accordance with their karmic merit.

And the burning of joss paper is sending gratitude for the ancestors, the "dead", who indeed are not dead, as their ambitions, desires, unfulfilled longings, health conditions, ailments, emotional temperaments, and physical traits express, here and now, in everyone in the clan. The more recent the dead, the stronger a living person feels the grasping clutch of the deceased's emotional attachments in their own life. The more distant the dead, the closer they are to spiritual fulfillment in the abiding reality beyond all transient forms. Indeed, the more distant the dead, the more they resemble the enlightened gods or the abiding serenity of nature.

On this contemplative day, my friend and I had been invited to two family fields. Of what age? How old is this family, the He clan? And how long have they been living on this same land? They had lived here before the Revolution, when this family land became state-owned land. And they had courageously remained here through the Red Guard atrocities, when people, I am told, tore out the largest trees of the gravesites, doing their best to destroy everything traditional. It is quite easy to kill a tree, but an act of supreme strength to maintain a familial continuity for centuries. Bravo!

This large and courageous clan piled into cars and SUVs and headed out to the best restaurant in town. And in a large room absolutely filled with people of every age, we ate, we toasted, we drank, and were fulfilled.

I thought that this was the end of the ceremonies. What more could there be?

We piled back into the SUV and headed to a town temple Wen Ping had pointed out on the way to the restaurant. It had an elevated statue in front of its huge outer wall. "Who is that?" I asked.

"He Tang," Wen Ping answered. "He is a great ancestor."

Apparently this was a temple dedicated in He Tang's honor. And as the SUV drove behind the outer wall, what a temple! A traditional opera stage bolstered the inside of the outer wall and faced a small open-air auditorium. Behind this was an inner temple, a stone bridge over a moat, a small pavilion, steles, and a large temple.

Standing next to a stele that commemorated He Tang's achievements, Wen Ping explained, "He Tang was born in the Ming Dynasty. He served as the teacher for a Qing Dynasty emperor."

"Your ancestor?"

"Yes."

The ground floor of the temple housed a huge statue and altar to He Tang. An illustrated calligraphic scroll along the left wall related the story of He Tang's life. I was briefly reminded of visiting the Cathedral of St. Francis in Assisi and seeing Giotto's frescos of

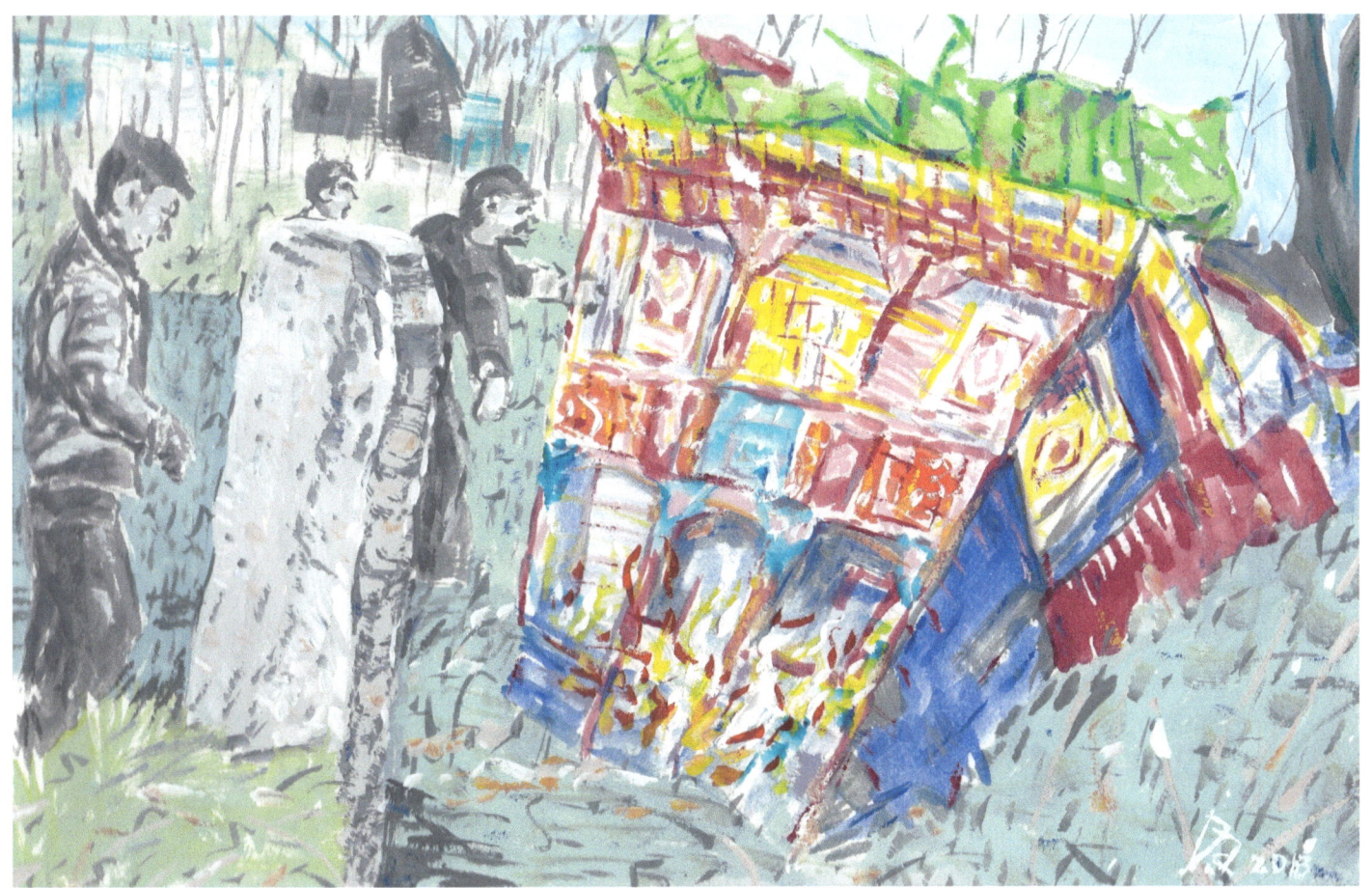

Paper Mansion For Ancestors During Ching Ming Festival

2018
Gouache on paper
9.625 x 5.75 in.   (25.4 x 15.87 cm.)

the life of St. Francis. Here too was a life story worthy of being told and retold by inspired generations.

The upper story of the temple was locked, but a caretaker opened it for Wen Ping and his family. The walls of the upper story are absolutely covered with illustrated calligraphic scrolls. Each one depicts an episode in the life of He Tang. The first one shows He Tang changing the temperament of belligerent students through the wisdom of his teachings. In the second scroll he is seen educating a young prince. The text reminds educators to be compassionate yet firm. The third scroll shows He Tang instructing men working on a timber roof beam. And so on around the walls in paintings and text that could easily fill a book.

At one end of the room is an altar to the female Taoist Immortal, He Xian Gu. Wen Ping casually mentions, "Oh, yeah. She is part of our family."

"You have one of the Taoist Immortals in your family?" I asked.

"Yeah."

I was speechless and utterly stupefied.

The folklore tradition of the Taoist immortals in China is similar to the European tradition of saint stories.

They are both hagiographies (spiritual biographies) and tales of local villagers encountering these miraculous human exemplars. Lady He was born over a thousand years ago, during the Tang Dynasty. Villagers were astounded by the six long golden hairs growing from the crown of her infant head. As a child, Lady He was taught the Taoist arts in vivid nighttime dreams. And during the day she practiced the medicinal, alchemical, and longevity practices she learned in dream transmissions from spiritual elders. Legends tell of her yogic accomplishments and spiritual powers. China's singular empress, Wu Zetian, sought to learn the techniques of immortality from her, but Lady He would always vanish like the reflection of the moon seemingly captured in a cup of water.

Afterward we visited Wen Ping's birth house and met his cousins and their families who lived nearby. One cousin's job was to build roof beams exactly like we had seen in the scroll paintings of He Tang. Bill remarked to Wen Ping, "You are a teacher, just like He Tang. Your cousin builds roof beams. I see the continuity of your family traditions."

The houses in this section of the village were very old. Mortared bricks were used for structural walls, unmortared bricks for much else, providing versatility to landscaping as well as raw materials for future need. I was amazed by the elegance of the tiled roofs. The house that Wen Ping was born in is now abandoned. A house nearby was built by his father, which again, it had the same timber roof beam as depicted in the scroll of He Tang.

Our rapidly modernizing age is characterized by a global loss of traditional culture. People of every nation struggle to compete in a global economy that has a shared materialistic worldview characterized by resource management. As elsewhere, many of China's traditions are disappearing.

And yet the hands of the living clasp those of their forefathers and on and on and on through time. What gratitude and love must extend through these strong arms back in time, an accomplishment truly befitting the family of the miraculous Lady He. This family, like others all across China, escaped the grasping demands of impersonal authority, like Empress Wu's clutching after immortality. If not immortality itself, ancestor devotion is at least a form of continuity as deep as cellular biology and as ancient as the earliest burial traditions that love sustains to this very day.

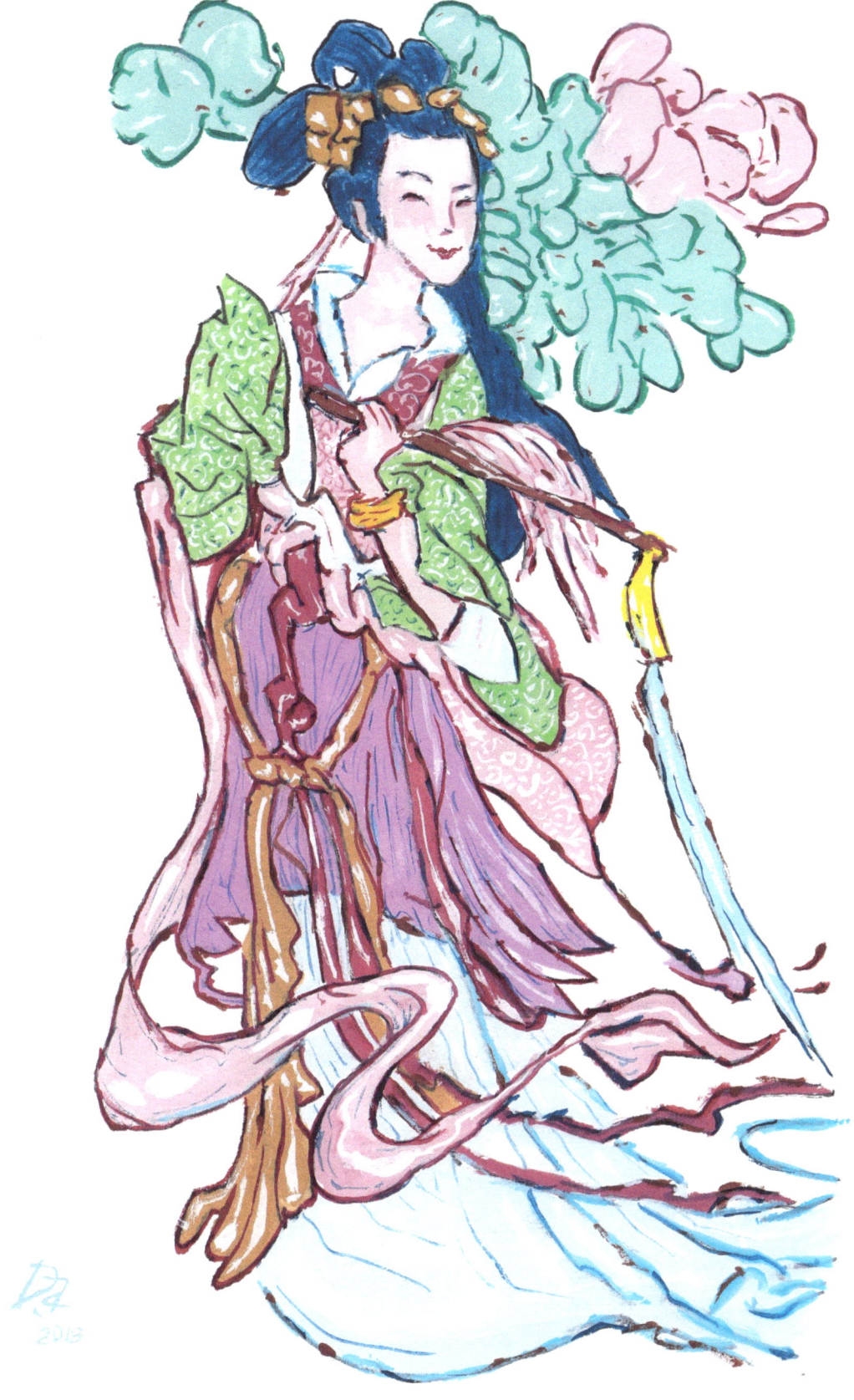

Lady He (He Xiangu) of the Eight Immortals

2018
Gouache on paper
8.27 X 11.7 in.   (27.3 x 18.41 cm.)

CONTEMPORARY AMERICAN EXPATRIATE PAINTER SERIES

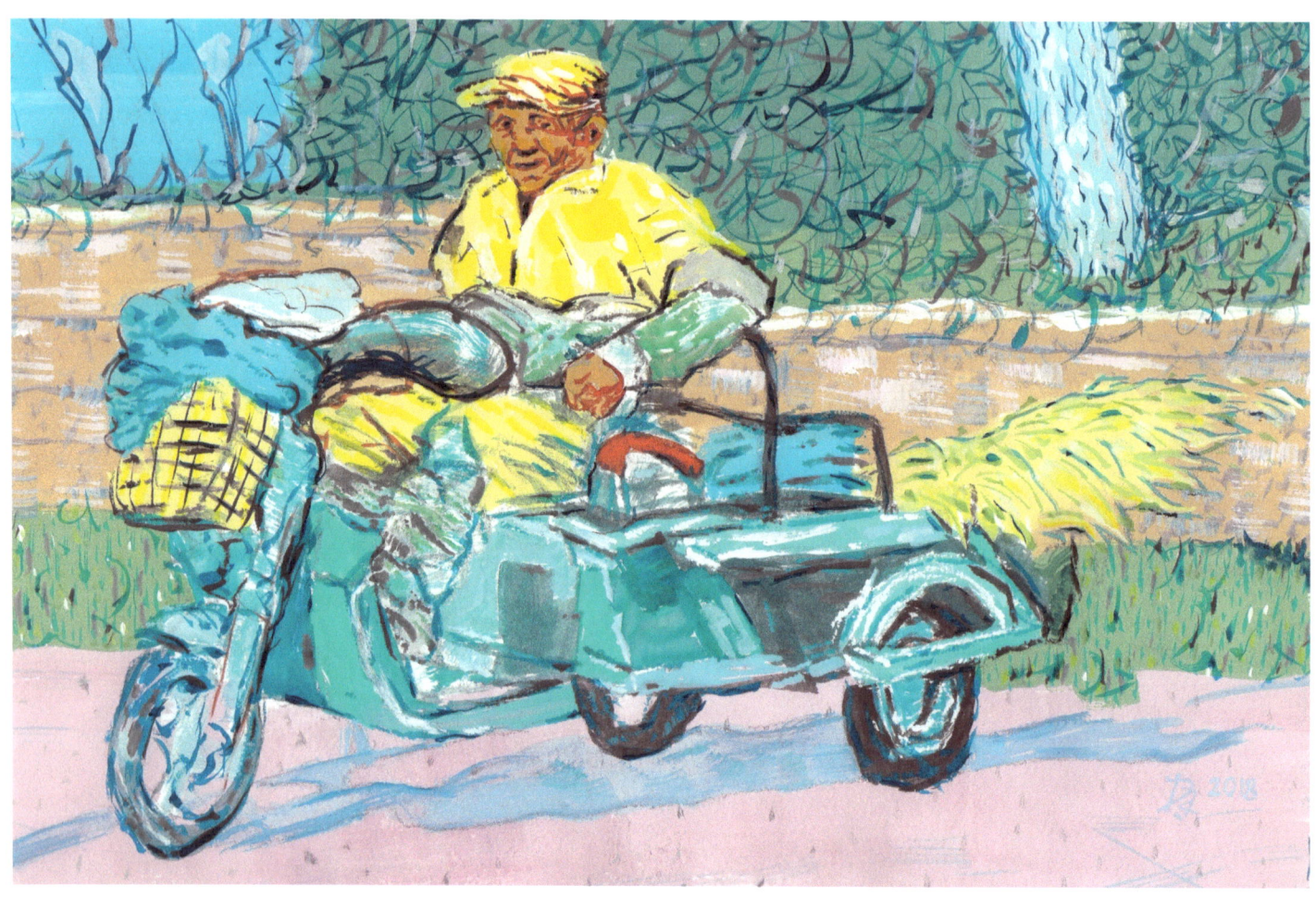

Chinese Garuda

2018
Gouache on paper
10.25 x 6.75 in.   (26 x 17.14 cm.)

DAVE ALBER: TRAVEL ART 2018: PART 1: INTIMATIONS

Comic: Bedding Shanghai

2018
Gouache on paper, Photoshop
Each page is 8.26 x 11.29 in.   (21 x 28.67 cm.)

Dave Alber's comic "Bedding Shanghai" was featured in the annual **Shanghai Erotic Fiction Contest**, which was part of the **Shanghai International Literary Festival** sponsored by **That's Shanghai Magazine**.

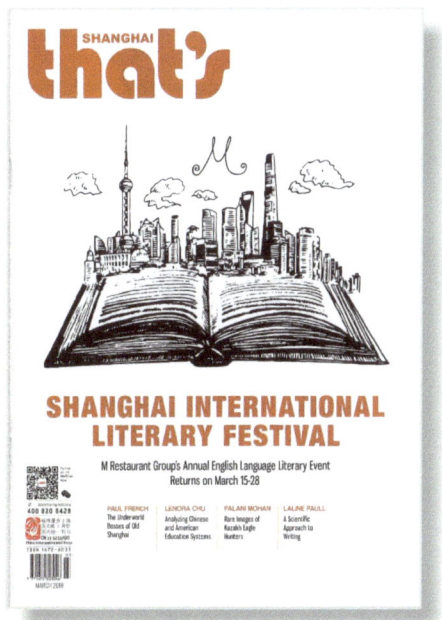

"The effort that Dave put into making 'Bedding Shanghai'… it's just wonderful."

Osamah Sami
Lit Fest Author

"This is our seventh Erotic Fiction Competition, going on seven years, and Dave Alber has added a whole new element to it."

Ned Kelly
Editor of That's Shanghai Magazine

"Very beautifully drawn. 'Separated by fluid, conjoined by fluid' is the most poetic description of Pudong and Puxi that I've ever heard. I also like the line, 'Thrusting, thrusting, thrusting' — a very simple description of three Shanghai landmarks. Simple and effective."

Erica Martin
Arts Editor at That's Shanghai Magazine
http://www.thatsmags.com/shanghai/post?author=Erica%20Martin

"Honestly, I have thought so much about Puxi and Pudong, but I've never thought about it like this. The visuals on that page, the breasts swelling, the Puxi and Pudong breasts. I can't even. So much effort. Thank you for sharing this with us. What a gift."

Clara Davis
Founder of Unravel
http://unravellive.com

21

CONTEMPORARY AMERICAN EXPATRIATE PAINTER SERIES

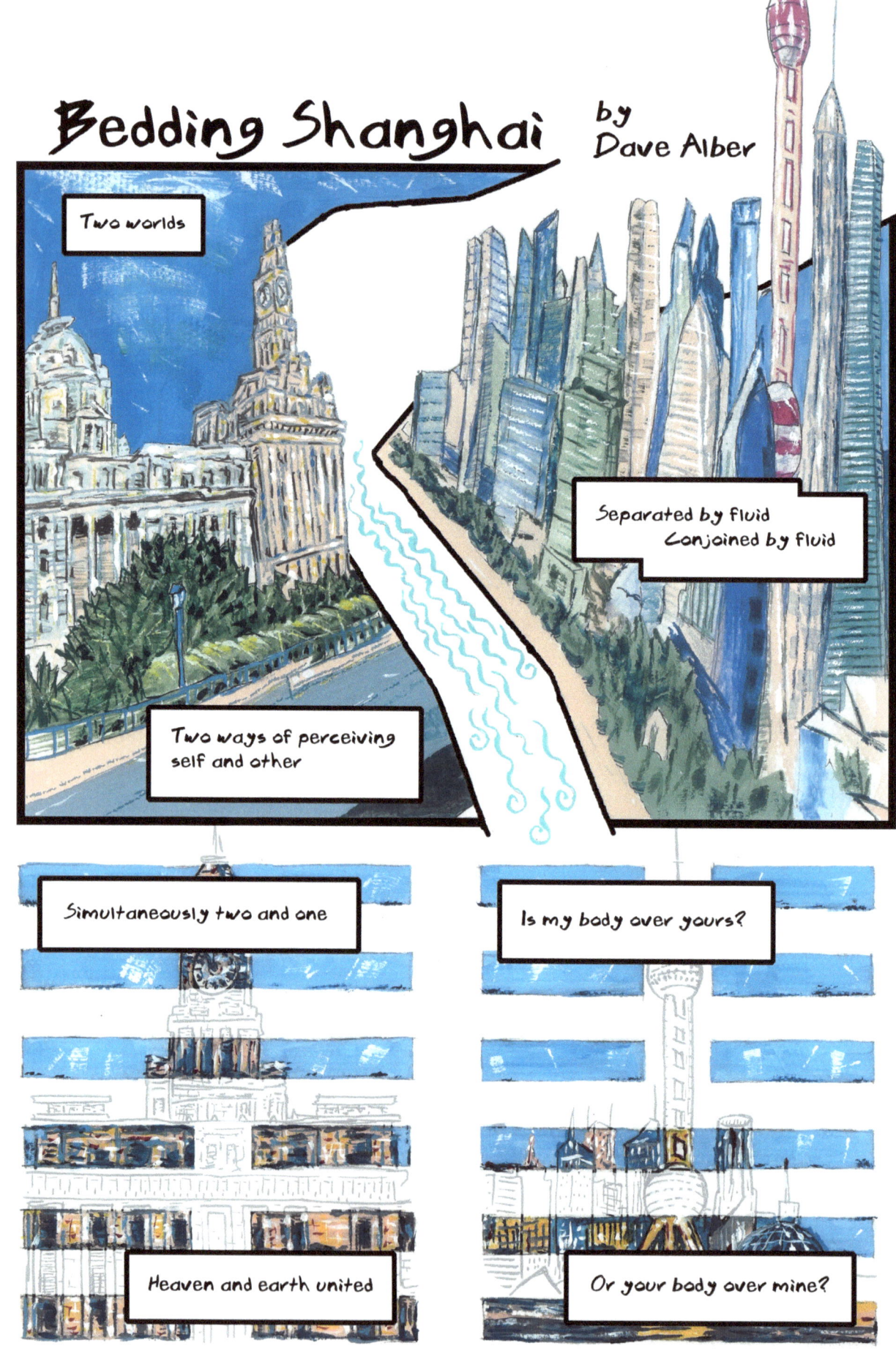

DAVE ALBER: TRAVEL ART 2018: PART 1: INTIMATIONS

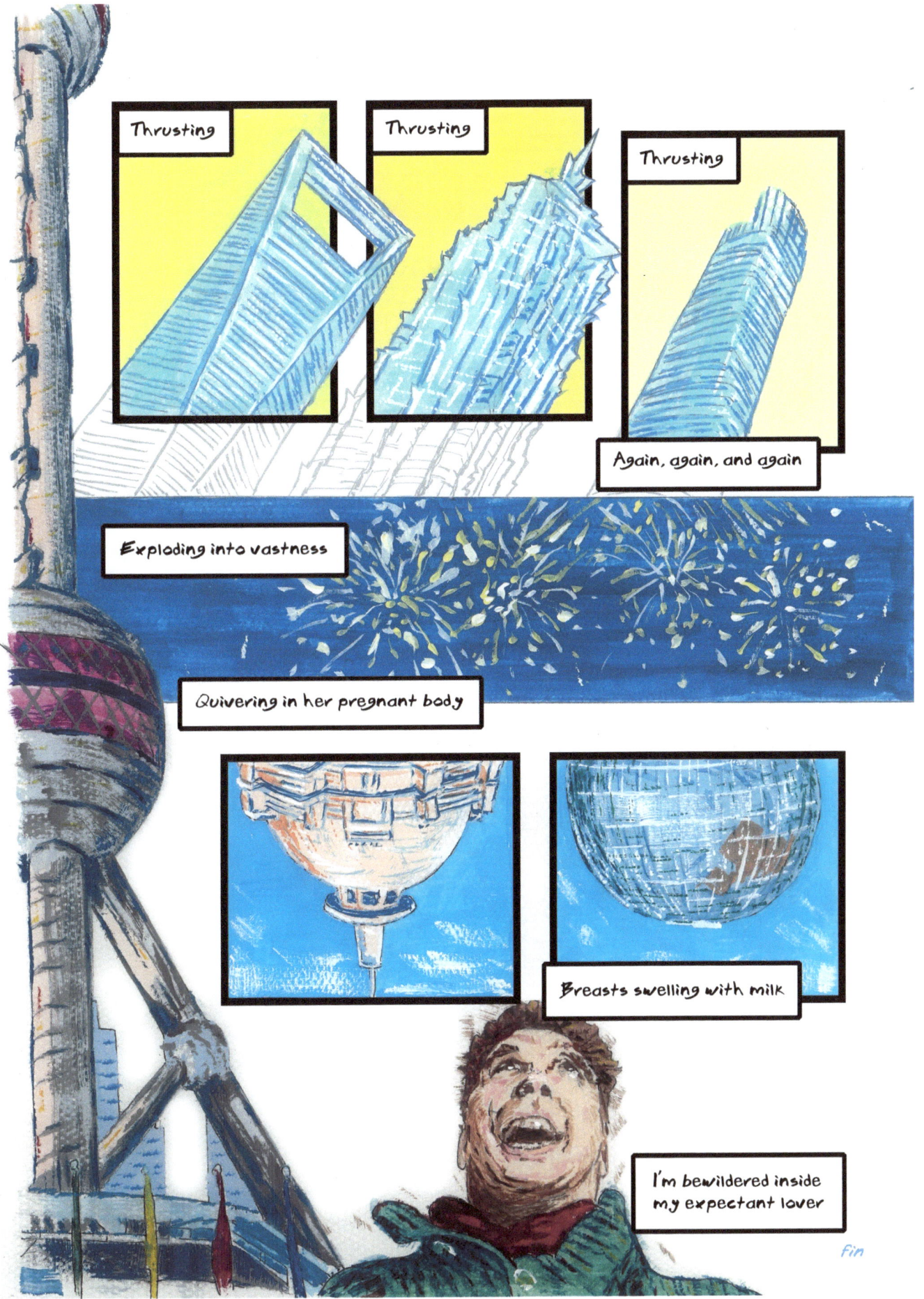

CONTEMPORARY AMERICAN EXPATRIATE PAINTER SERIES

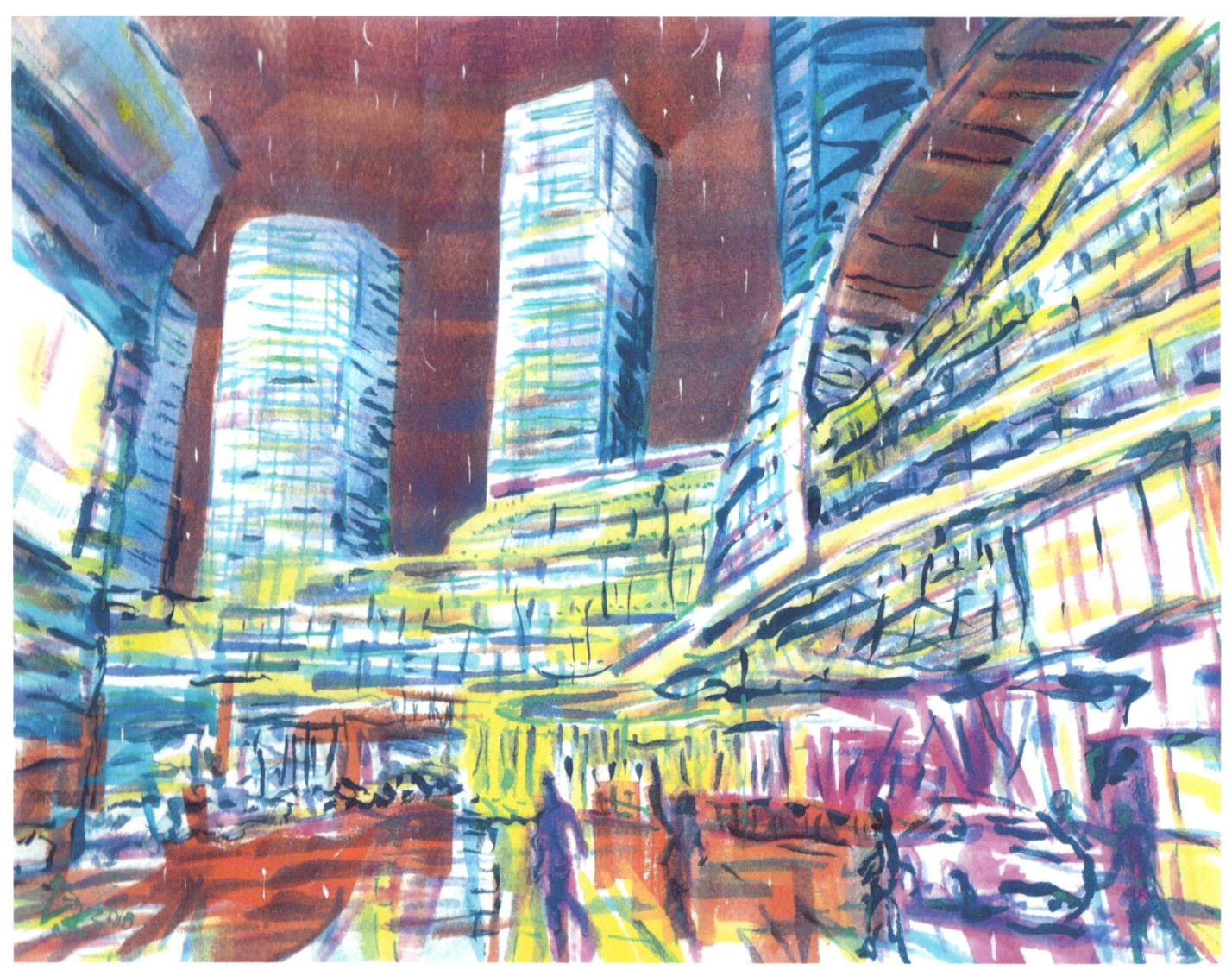

Suzhou Center Mall in the Rain, East Side

2018
Gouache on paper
10 x 7.61 in   (25.4 x 19.33 cm.)

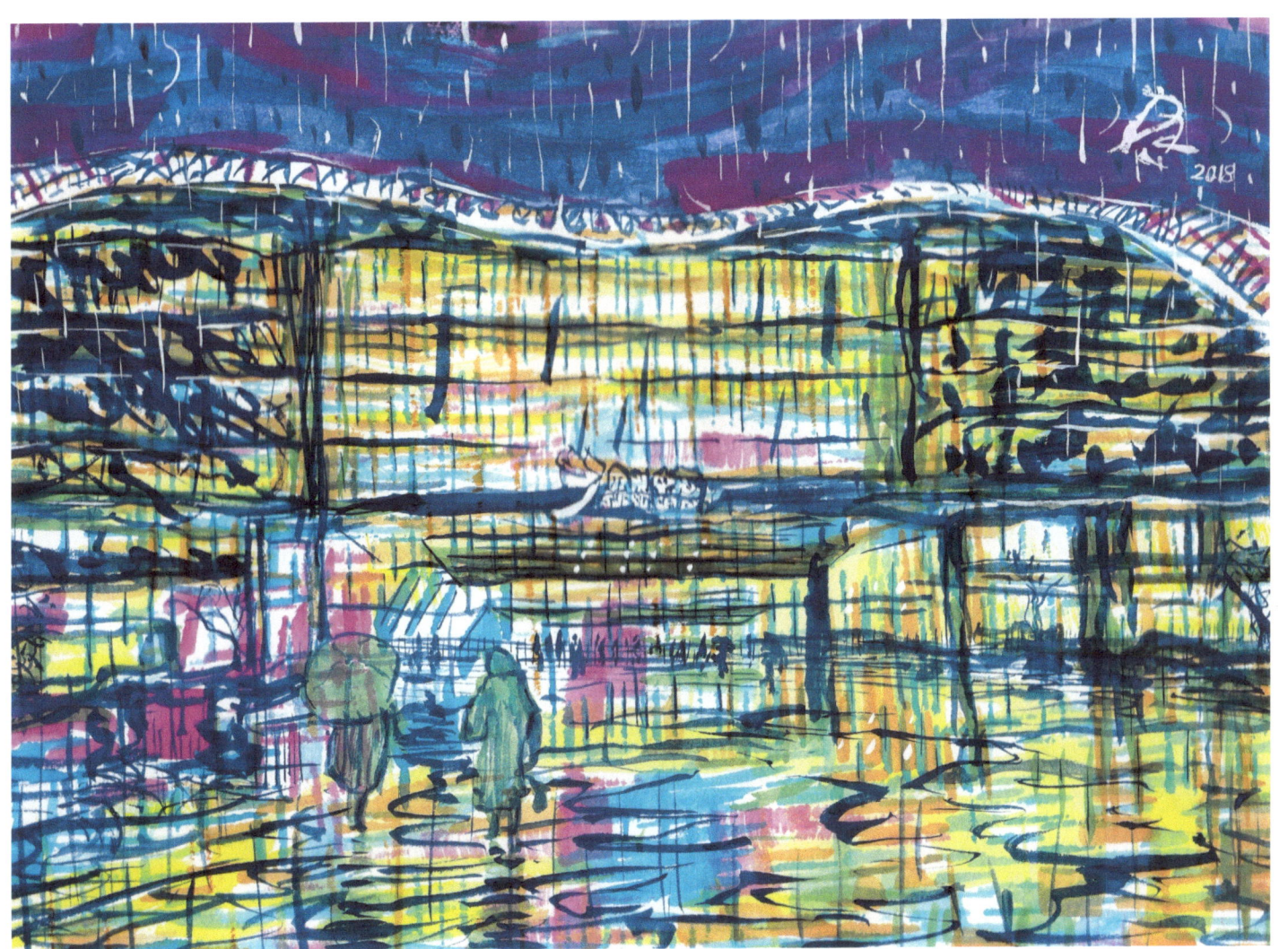

Suzhou Center Mall in the Rain, East Entrance

2018
Gouache on paper
9.96 x 7.1 in.   (25.3 x 18 cm.)

CONTEMPORARY AMERICAN EXPATRIATE PAINTER SERIES

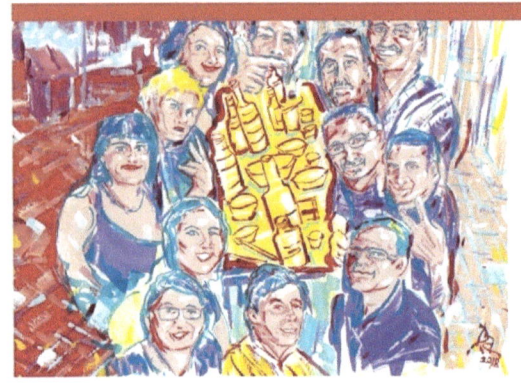

"Getting Social at Suzhou's Night Market" is an article published in the Suzhou Review on May 28, 2018. **Eating With Friends at Dachengfang Guanqian Night Market, Suzhou, China** is a gouache illustration featured in the article.

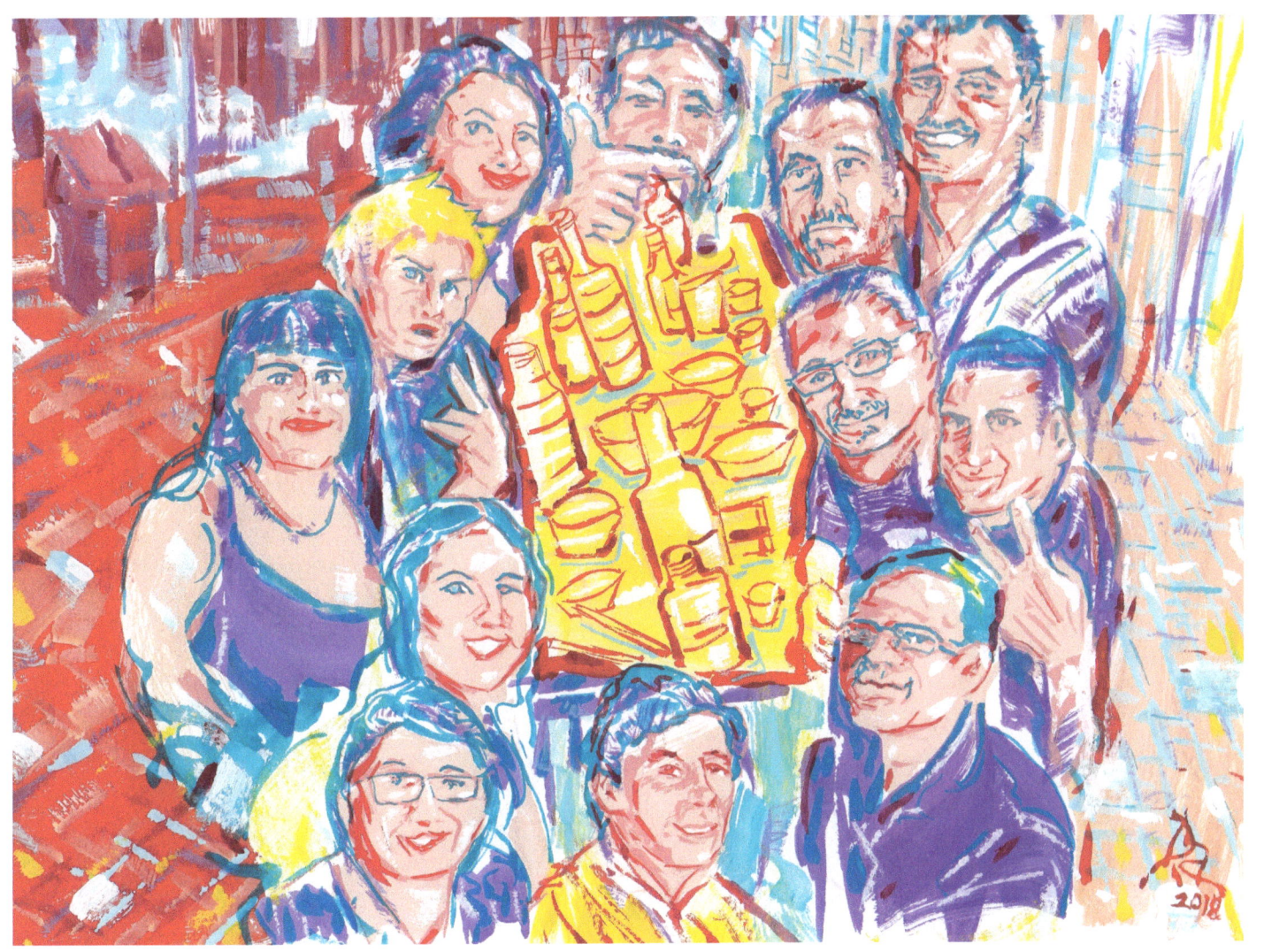

Eating With Friends at Dachengfang Guanqian Night Market, Suzhou, China

2018
Gouache on paper
12 x 10 in.   (30.48 x 25.4 cm.)

CONTEMPORARY AMERICAN EXPATRIATE PAINTER SERIES

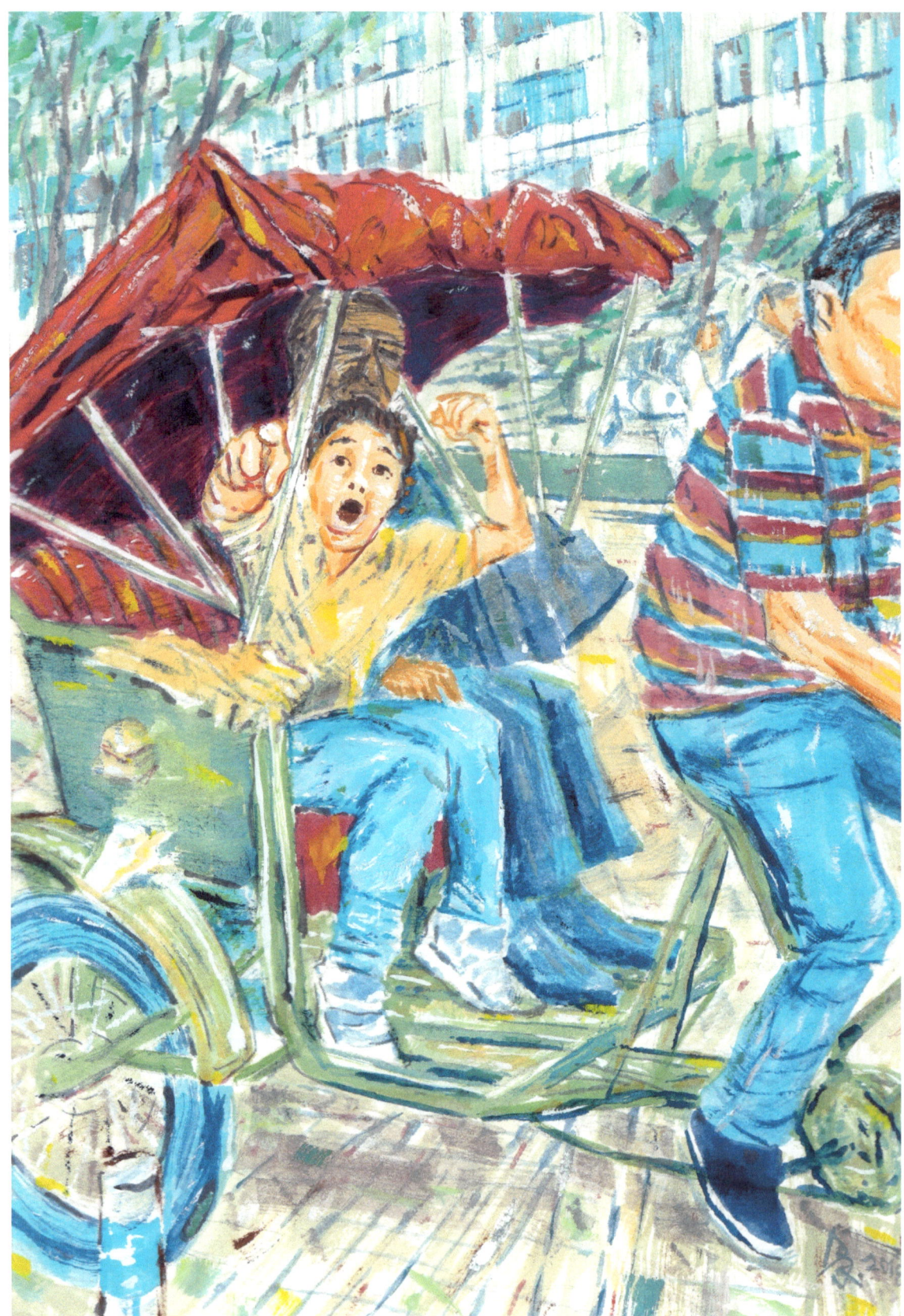

"WAIGUARAN!"

2018
Gouache on paper
7.1 x 10 in.   (18 x 25.4 cm.)

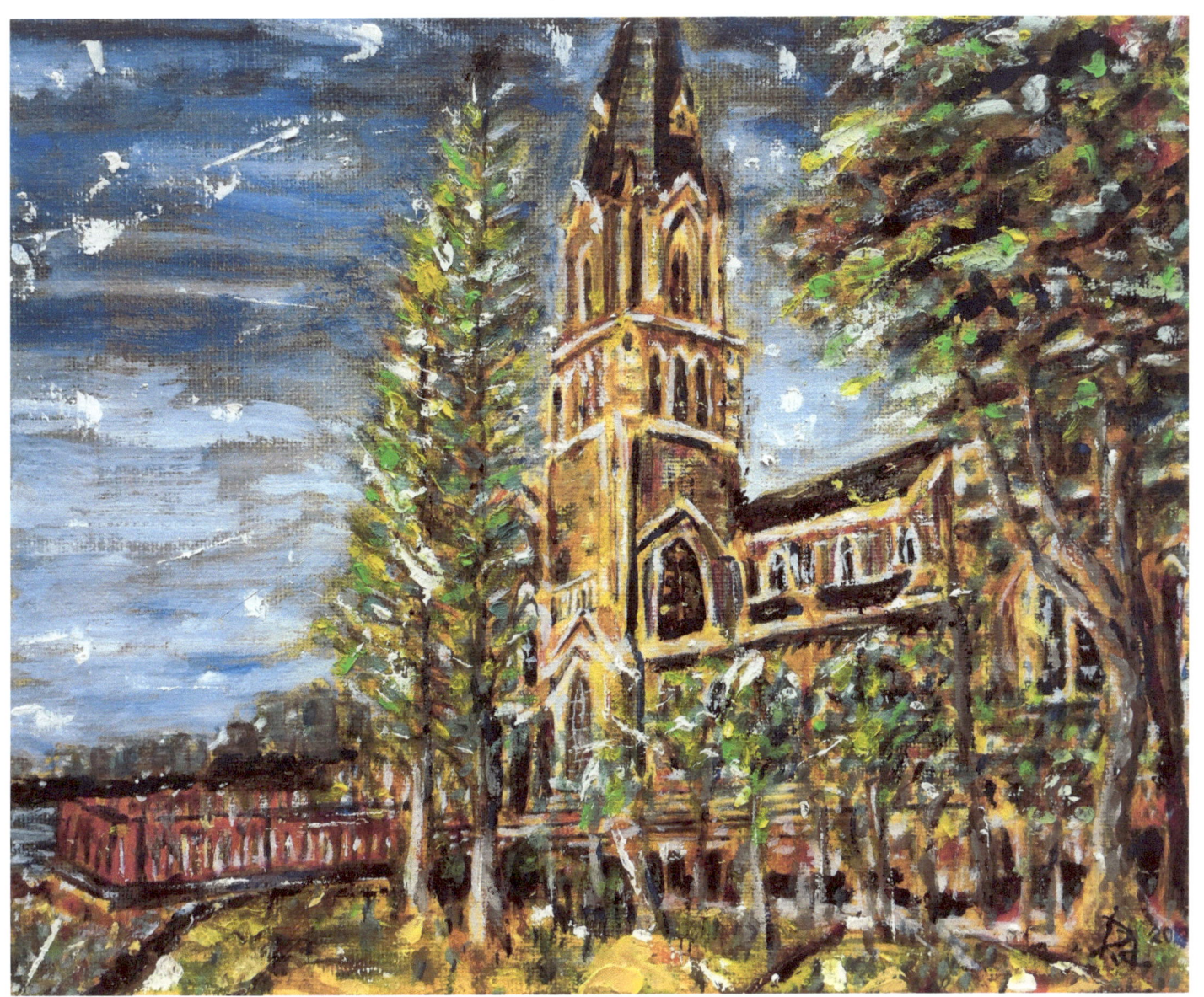

Dushu Lake Church (Suzhou, China)

2018
Oil on canvas
12 x 10 in.   (30.5 x 25.4 cm.)

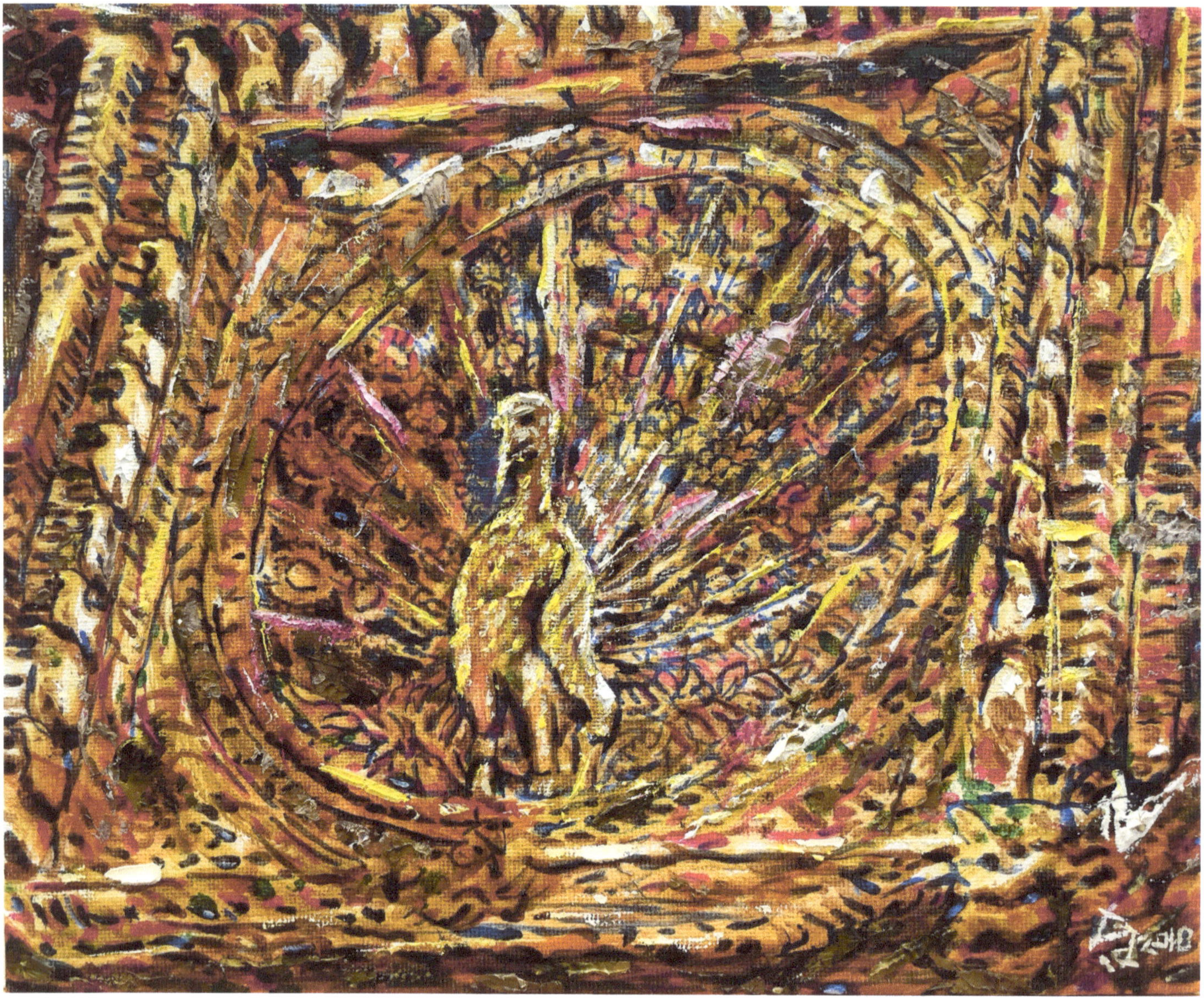

CONTEMPORARY AMERICAN EXPATRIATE PAINTER SERIES

Peacock Window (Bhaktapur, Nepal)

2018
Oil on canvas
12 x 10 in.   (30.5 x 25.4 cm.)

"The Peacock Shop in Bhaktapur, Nepal: An Interview with Suyog Prajapati at The Peacock Shop" appeared online in the **Nepali Renaissance** blog. The article contains the painting **Peacock Window (Bhaktapur, Nepal)**.

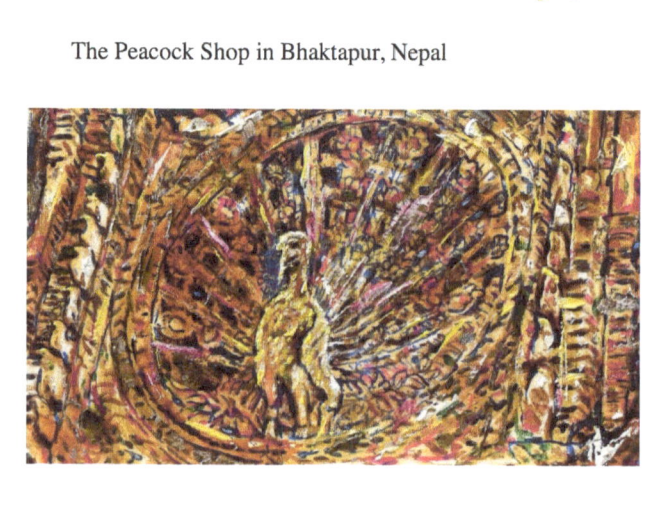

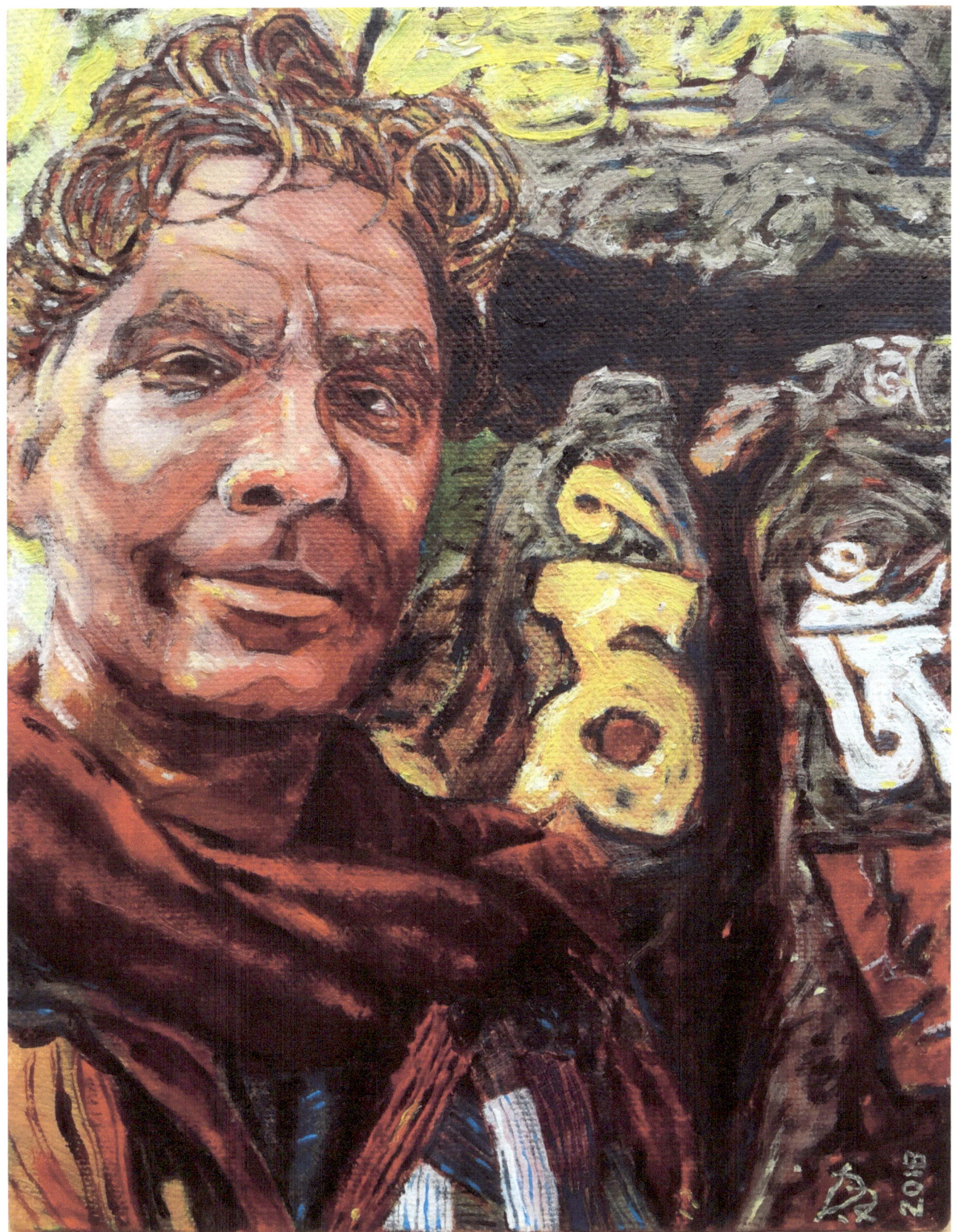

Dave Alber, Self-Portrait at Swayambunath, Kathmandu, Nepal

2018
Oil on canvas
9.375 x 11.75 in.   (23.81 x 29.84 cm.)

CONTEMPORARY AMERICAN EXPATRIATE PAINTER SERIES

Commission a portrait of someone you love

Immortalize your love in a portrait...
connect and order your portrait now.

Portrait Paintings in Chinese Ink

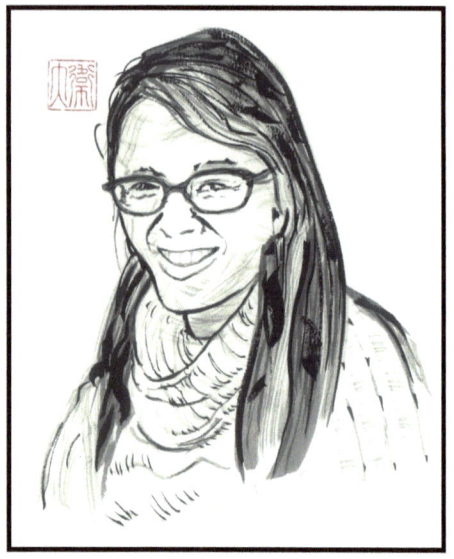
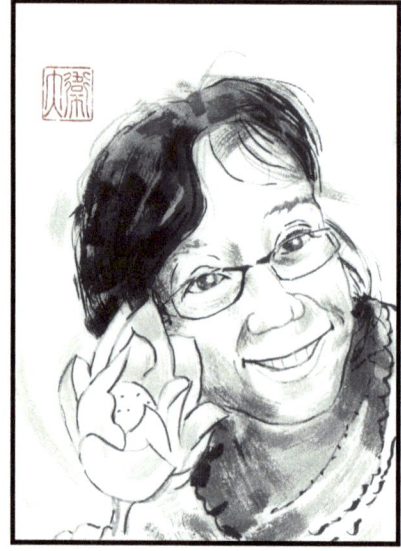
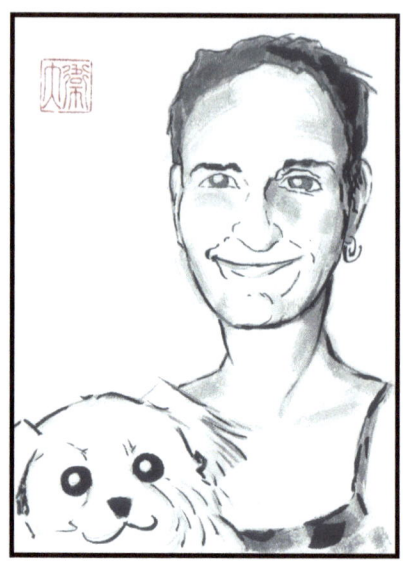

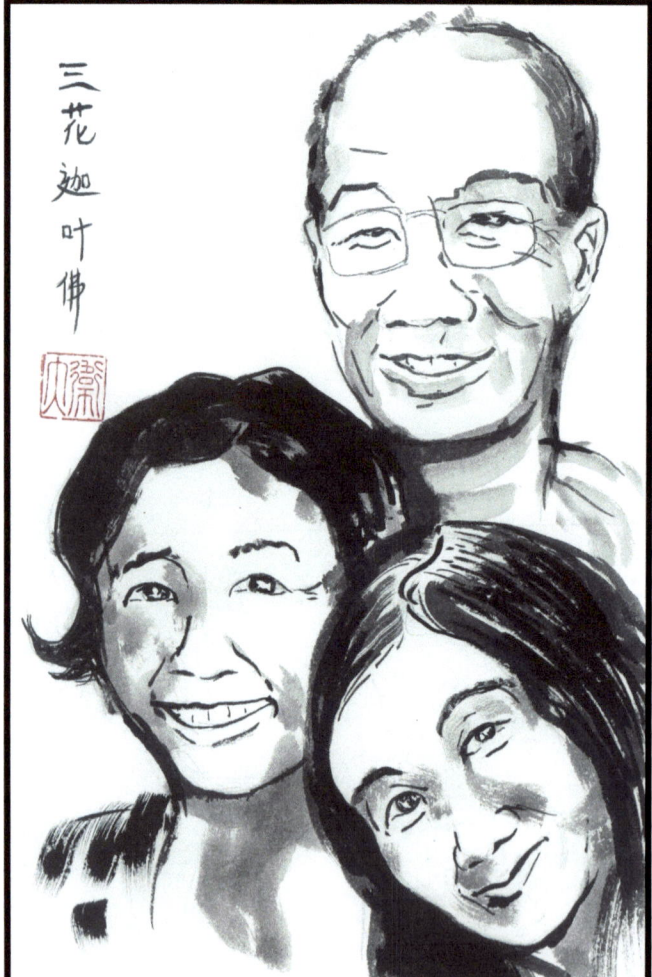

"The portrait makes me feel warm. The figures are lively with their smiles. I can see the happiness, innocence, wisdom, and kindness on their faces. These paintings can keep you open-minded and uplift your frequency. They contain the painter's perception of life, which are always showing you an opportunity to see it's possible to express who you are and be your own style. What's the value of paintings which are able to encourage and inspire you to open your own unique adventure of life?"

"Dave, the painter, has grasped the essence of Chinese ink painting and well-practiced it into these paintings. This combination of Western background and Eastern arts is quite profound and fantastic."

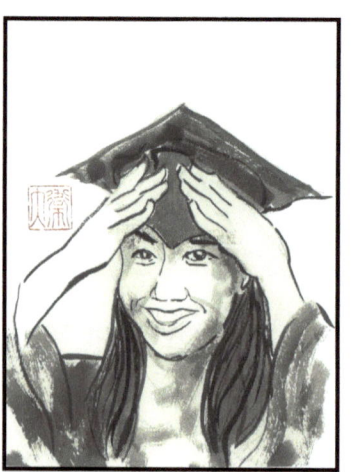
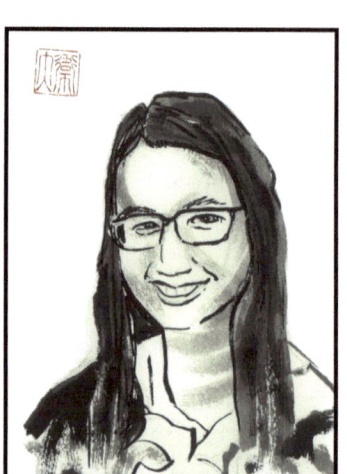

www.ingramcontent.com/pod-product-compliance
Lightning Source LLC
Chambersburg PA
CBHW051823210526
45473CB00005B/1715